MUSEUM FRIEDER BURDA
BADEN-BADEN

MUSEUM BARBERINI
POTSDAM

The exhibition is held under the patronage of
Federal President Frank-Walter Steinmeier.

Avant-Garde

Max Liebermann and Impressionism in Germany

Exhibition and catalog:
Ortrud Westheider and Daniel Zamani
with Valentina Plotnikova and Christiane Righetti

Edited by
Michael Philipp
Nerina Santorius
Ortrud Westheider
Daniel Zamani

With contributions by
Alexander Bastek
Karoline Feulner
Valentina Plotnikova
Christiane Righetti
Barbara Schaefer
Lucy Wasensteiner
Ortrud Westheider
Daniel Zamani

PRESTEL Munich · London · New York

Contents

Foreword

There is no stupider claim than the one we . . . read and hear daily: that Naturalism is dead. For all art is based on nature, and everything lasting in it is nature. Not only that which surrounds the artist, but above all his own nature. How he, the artist, views the world, with his internal and external senses—I call that his imagination—the forming of this, his imagination, is his art. As a painter, I proceed from vision, and so I am interested exclusively in the forming imagination, while for me the creative imagination in the work of art is an axiom. It is divine inspiration, with which we can come to grips only by way of pure thought (if we can come to grips with it at all). But we may hope to trace the workings of the forming imagination through psychological and empirical means. Or in other words: we are permitted to want to try, through technique, to explain the spirit that engendered the work.

Max Liebermann, 1916

In the evolution of German Impressionism, the gaze over to France played a crucial role from the beginning. Max Liebermann and numerous other painters derived inspiration from the works of their French colleagues, with which they could familiarize themselves on extended trips to Paris. The first presentation of French Impressionism in Germany was in Berlin in October 1883. Galerie Fritz Gurlitt showed sixteen paintings by Édouard Manet, Claude Monet, Camille Pissarro, and Alfred Sisley, of which ten works were from the holdings of husband-and-wife collectors Carl and Felicie Bernstein. It was followed in the 1890s by exhibitions in Munich and Weimar. Around the turn of the century, the Berlin Secession and Galerie Paul Cassirer regularly exhibited paintings such as Claude Monet's *Impression, Sunrise* and Édouard Manet's *Luncheon on the Grass* (figs. p. 23), which were still regarded as scandalous even in France.

In Germany, these exhibitions mobilized the opposition to the national renewal of art that the emperor had declared. To the latter's outrage, the director of the Nationalgalerie, art historian Hugo von Tschudi, had already acquired significant modern French paintings in the 1890s. Liebermann assembled an important collection in this field that guests to his villa on the Wannsee could admire. Much like Monet in Giverny, he put in an elaborately tended garden from 1909 onward; the splendid colors of its flowers became a major motif of his late Impressionist work (see cats. 117–32).

The show *Avant-Garde: Max Liebermann and Impressionism in Germany* not only shows Liebermann as a central artist of that movement but also sheds light on his extraordinary influence as a collector, exhibition organizer, and mentor. In the archconservative German Empire, the Jewish painter also served as president of the Berlin Secession and was a courageous voice for progress, internationality, and innovation—and an important figure in the increasingly intense dialogue with France. In the wake of the Exposition Universelle of 1889, the French government awarded Liebermann a medal of honor and admitted him to the prestigious Société des Beaux-Arts. Five years later, his painting *Beer Garden in Brannenburg* (cat. 28) was acquired for the Musée du Luxembourg in Paris. That was followed in 1896 by his admission to the French Legion of Honor.

Liebermann died two years after power was transferred to the Nazis, who abruptly ended developments in modern painting in Germany. His widow, Martha Liebermann, committed suicide in 1943, a few days before she was to be deported to the Theresienstadt concentration camp. Their daughter, Käthe, and young granddaughter, Maria, had fled to exile in the United States in 1938. Liebermann's extensive collection of French Impressionist painting has since been scattered to the winds, and much of it is now in collections on the other side of the Atlantic. His villa on the Wannsee is not only an important cultural legacy but also a political memorial.

The exhibition *Avant-Garde: Max Liebermann and Impressionism in Germany* pays tribute to Liebermann's contribution to German art and culture within a broadened context of the Impressionist movement. In addition to painters who have long since occupied a solid position within the canon, such as Lovis Corinth, Max Slevogt, and Fritz von Uhde, it also looks at artists whose contribution deserves to be rediscovered, including Philipp Franck, Friedrich Kallmorgen, Gotthardt Kuehl, Heinrich Eduard Linde-Walther, Lesser Ury, and Max Uth. A focused group of important works by women painters who were able to establish themselves as artists in the German Empire but have largely been forgotten today should also be emphasized: Charlotte Berend-Corinth, Emilie von Hallavanya, Dora Hitz, Sabine Lepsius, Maria Slavona, and Eva Stort.

With more than 130 works from more than sixty international collections, this show is one of the largest exhibitions ever dedicated to the evolution of German Impressionism. With works by more than twenty artists, it reflects on the movement's enormous diversity, spanning a chronological arc from the 1880s to the 1930s. Thematically, the show is dedicated to the impulses coming from France and their resonance chamber in Germany before and after World War I. After the turn of the century, the nation-states of the nineteenth century shared emancipation efforts and modernization movements. Technological progress in production, communication, and mobility and lively research in the natural sciences contributed to a new liberality in Europe. The plein-air painting style of Impressionism and its new themes of the modern metropolis and bourgeois leisure activities were paradigmatic of this era of innovation.

The Museum Barberini, which has 115 Impressionist and Postimpressionist paintings from the Hasso Plattner Collection in its permanent exhibition, has long since dedicated its exhibition program to French and international Impressionism. In 2019 it presented the show *Impressionism in Russia: Dawn of the Avant-Garde*. In 2020 the exhibition *Clouds and Light: Impressionism in Holland* followed. Including an exhibition on Impressionism in Germany in this series means shedding light on the works of our own art history with a fresh distance and from the perspective of internationality.

The exhibition *Impressionism in Russia* was already a cooperation with the Museum Frieder Burda, and we are extraordinarily pleased that the two institutions and their highly engaged teams have come together again for this project. At the Museum Frieder Burda, the exhibition creates a bridge between Liebermann's many paintings of gardens and Baden-Baden's historical tradition in horticulture and landscape design—a focus of the city exemplified by its famous Lichtentaler Allee, in whose park landscape the museum's gleaming white building by Richard Meier is harmoniously integrated. The lushly planted

Gönneranlage, a park designed, like Liebermann's artist's garden of 1909, according to the ideas of the garden reform movement, was, like all the city's beds, blooming in 2025 with colors from the bright palette of Liebermann's Wannsee paintings. For that, we owe thanks to Markus Brunsing, director of Baden-Baden's Department of Parks.

A scholarly symposium held at the Museum Barberini on December 11, 2024, prepared the ground for the exhibition *Avant-Garde: Max Liebermann and Impressionism in Germany* and the accompanying catalog. We would like to thank all the authors for their lectures, which can be read in the form of extensive essays in this volume. We also thank Valentina Plotnikova for her chapter introductions and her exemplary management of the catalog editing. As a curatorial assistant in Potsdam, she helped develop this ambitious project from the beginning and with Christiane Righetti in Baden-Baden helped implement it successfully. We are both indebted to the many collections that made works available for the exhibitions, including icons of German Impressionism such as Liebermann's *Samson and Delilah* (cat. 111) from the Städel Museum in Frankfurt am Main, Corinth's *Woman at the Goldfish Tank* (cat. 66) from the Belvedere in Vienna, Slevogt's *The Champagne Aria* (cat. 115) from the Staatsgalerie Stuttgart and *Francisco d'Andrade as Don Giovanni in Mozart's Opera* (cat. 116) from the Alte Nationalgalerie in Berlin, and Uhde's *Children's Room* (cat. 87) from the Hamburger Kunsthalle, as well as numerous important works from private collections that are not ordinarily accessible to the public. Our sincere gratitude is also due to Federal President Frank-Walter Steinmeier, who kindly accepted our invitation to take over the patronage of this large survey exhibition.

We wish our visitors joy and stimulation when they plunge into the colorful pictorial worlds of Max Liebermann and his colleagues: paintings that impressively demonstrate the high quality and emotional power of Impressionism in Germany.

Ortrud Westheider
Director
Museum Barberini,
Potsdam

Daniel Zamani
Artistic Director
Museum Frieder Burda,
Baden-Baden

Acknowledgments

For the advice and assistance provided in putting together the exhibition and catalog, our heartfelt thanks are due to Marion Ackermann, Sylvain Amic, Stefanie Arz, Gernot Barounig, Anne Barz, Alexander Bastek, Susanne Baunach, Leonie Beiersdorf, Hetty Berg, Heike Biedermann, Markus Bertsch, Dirk Boll, Markus Brunsing, Frédéric Bußmann, Freya Cazalet, Anke Darrelmann, Philipp Demandt, Anja Dorn, Sandra Dreher, Bernd Ebert, Lucy Economakis, Alexander Eiling, Nadine Engel, Martin Faass, Karoline Feulner, Barbara Forest, Ralph Gleis, Christine Goerlipp, Peter Gorschlüter, Christoph Grunenberg, Dorothee Hansen, Birgit Heide, Sebastian Heimberg, Andreas Henning, Frieder Hepp, Inge Herold, Katrin Hippel, Johan Holten, Julia Höner, Stefan Hörter, Marcus Andrew Hurttig, Anette Hüsch, Toby Kamps, Micaela Kapitzky, Alexander Klar, Gudrun Klemm, Felix Krämer, Viktoria Bernadette Krieger, Christiane Lange, Ulrich Luckhardt, Annette Ludwig, Bernhard Maaz, Roland Mönig, Ruth Oberhand, Kristine von Oehsen, Paul Perrin, Estelle Pietrzyk, Sophie Plagemann, Isolde Pludermacher, Stella Rollig, Herbert W. Rott, Nora Rüsenberg, Barbara Schaefer, Stephan Scherer, Sabine Maria Schmidt, Hemma Schmutz, Dieter Scholz, Eva Susanne Schweizer, Katrin Steffen, Anna Storm, Florian Struckmeier, Florence Thurmes, Hilke Wagner, Lucy Wasensteiner, Stefan Weppelmann, Evelyn Wöldicke, Richard Lee Wilding, and Ulrike Wolff-Thomsen.

Lenders

Museum Kunst der Westküste, Alkersum/Föhr
Staatliche Museen zu Berlin, Nationalgalerie
Jüdisches Museum Berlin
Stiftung Stadtmuseum Berlin
Kunsthalle Bremen—Der Kunstverein in Bremen
Kunstsammlungen Chemnitz
Wallraf-Richartz-Museum & Fondation Corboud, Cologne
Hessisches Landesmuseum Darmstadt
Albertinum, Staatliche Kunstsammlungen Dresden
Leopold-Hoesch-Museum, Düren
Museum Folkwang, Essen
Städel Museum, Frankfurt am Main
Kunstmuseum Gelsenkirchen
Hamburger Kunsthalle
Niedersächsisches Landesmuseum Hannover
Kurpfälzisches Museum Heidelberg
Staatliche Kunsthalle Karlsruhe
Museum der bildenden Künste Leipzig
Lentos Kunstmuseum Linz
Tate, London
Lübecker Museen. Museum Behnhaus Drägerhaus
Museo Nacional Thyssen-Bornemisza, Carmen Thyssen Collection, Madrid
Landesmuseum Mainz
Kunsthalle Mannheim
Bayerische Staatsgemäldesammlungen, Munich—Neue Pinakothek
Städtische Galerie im Lenbachhaus und Kunstbau, Munich
Musée d'Orsay, Paris
Kunstforum Ostdeutsche Galerie, Regensburg
Arp Museum Bahnhof Rolandseck, Remagen, courtesy private collection, Cologne
Museum für Kunst und Kulturgeschichte Schloss Gottorf, Schleswig
Kunstmuseum Solothurn, Dübi-Müller-Stiftung
Musée d'Art moderne et contemporain de Strasbourg
Staatsgalerie Stuttgart
Belvedere, Vienna
Klassik Stiftung Weimar
Stiftung Schlösschen im Hofgarten Wertheim
Museum Wiesbaden
Von der Heydt-Museum Wuppertal
Museum im Kulturspeicher, Würzburg
Kunsthaus Zürich

Galerie Bastian, Berlin
Hegenbarth Sammlung Berlin
Galerie von Negelein
Galerie Paffrath
David Ragusa Collection
Claus H. Wencke Collection
Dr. Matthias Wilkening Foundation
Private collection, Berlin
Private collection BRENNET GmbH
Private collection, Cologne, courtesy Galerie Paffrath
Private collection, Frankfurt am Main
Private collection, Germany
Private collection, courtesy Daxer & Marschall, Munich
Private collection, southern Germany

as well as numerous private lenders, who wish to remain anonymous

Ortrud Westheider

The First Avant-Garde
Impressionism in Germany

The revolt against Wilhelmine art in the 1890s and the first years of this century was in reality the beginning of the revolution. The fragility of the imperial system was sensed and attacked much earlier in art and literature than in politics.
Harry Graf Kessler, eulogy for Paul Cassirer, 1926[1]

In the nineteenth century, plein-air painting gave rise to a movement against academic art that amounted to a kind of artistic self-empowerment: direct observation took the place of compositional formulas, traditional narratives were supplanted by an interest in contemporary life, and subjective sensation found more immediate expression in color than in drawn line. The Impressionist painting of light broke with hitherto prevailing aesthetic norms and led to an art that resonated with the modern individual. Its audience was the emerging middle class in Western industrial nations, who at first embraced the new current only hesitantly and remained largely skeptical until the turn of the century, even in France. Incomprehension and scandal, however, fueled the interest of new actors: writers became art critics, publishers became art dealers, entrepreneurs became collectors. Reaction turned into partisanship: art historians such as Heinrich Wölfflin and artists such as Max Liebermann agreed that what they were experiencing was a revolution in art, an art that for the first time in history gave itself over to external appearances.[2] This artistic revolution drove the self-empowerment of the bourgeoisie. Supporters of modernism saw themselves as pioneers and adopted combative language and a military vocabulary.[3]

The following essay explores the paradoxical coexistence of both revolutionary and conservative elements in the development of modern art. It takes the concept of the "avant-garde," established in French art criticism of the 1880s in reference to Impressionism, and transfers it to German Impressionism and its circle of supporters. During the same period, advocates of French Impressionism also expressed sympathy for the German Naturalism of artists such as Max Liebermann; all anti-academic tendencies were subsumed under the umbrella of Secessionism. In France, the term *avant-garde* had established itself as a battle cry against the interpretative control over contemporary art exercised by the Académie des Beaux-Arts. In Germany, as in many other European countries, a similar opposition to academic convention was ultimately underwritten by the liberal bourgeoisie. Although Impressionism developed later in Germany than in France, it achieved success far more rapidly, giving rise to an international movement around 1900. Until the breakthrough of Expressionism in the early twentieth century, Impressionism was the first avant-garde in Germany.

The Synchronicity of the Asynchronous

French Impressionist painting arrived in Germany during the years of upheaval following the Franco-Prussian War of 1870–71. King Wilhelm I of Prussia had been crowned emperor of the German Empire in the palace of Versailles, and a new national state was created. The empire in Germany confronted the Third Republic established by the French national assembly. The war, the imperial proclamation, and the unification of the Reich led to an intensification of German nationalism that burdened the relationship between Germany and France for decades—and with it the reception of French Impressionism by conservative elites in Germany. For over forty years, German history painter Anton von Werner dominated artistic and cultural policy at court. From 1874 on—the year of the first Impressionist exhibition in Paris—he served as director of the Hochschule der bildenden Künste (Academy of Fine Arts) in Berlin, where he shaped artistic education in Germany until his death in 1915. Yet for all his resistance to modernism, the controversies he provoked fueled the interest in international art.

The formation of an artistic avant-garde was inseparably connected to the rise of the middle class. The decisive impulses for the modernization of painting arose from bourgeois educational institutions and the efforts of private supporters.[4] Even during the "pre-March period" (the years preceding the revolution of March 1848), art and artists' associations had already emerged as a counterweight to aristocratic collecting. Germany's decentralized structure allowed important art centers to develop in the former residential cities of Darmstadt, Dresden, Düsseldorf, Karlsruhe, Mannheim, Munich, Stuttgart, and Weimar, as well as in former imperial cities such as Cologne, Hamburg, and Leipzig. In contrast to France, whose uncontested capital was Paris, these competing regional metropolises generated important impulses.[5] The Munich Secession, founded in 1892 on the model of the Vienna Secession, constituted a first initiative with openness toward French Impressionism. The same year in Berlin, the group known as the Association of the XI was founded, followed in 1898 by the Berlin Secession.[6]

1
Édouard Manet,
In the Conservatory, 1878–79,
Alte Nationalgalerie, Berlin

After his appointment as director of the Nationalgalerie, Hugo von Tschudi traveled to Paris in 1896 with Max Liebermann, where he acquired the painting *In the Conservatory* by Édouard Manet (fig. 1). It was the first Impressionist work to enter a German museum collection. The purchase, which would define Impressionism in Germany, represents the synchronicity of the asynchronous: the Nationalgalerie, whose pediment inscription "Der deutschen Kunst" (To German Art) conveyed the idea of the unification of the empire, took the lead in European institutional art policy in 1896—the same year the government in Paris was still wrangling over French painter Gustave Caillebotte's bequest of his collection to the French government.

The interest in contemporary art on the part of the liberal bourgeoisie boosted the art market. In 1880 Fritz Gurlitt opened his gallery in Berlin, giving a forum to the anti-academic painting of Wilhelm Leibl, Max Liebermann, Franz Skarbina, Hans Thoma, Wilhelm Trübner, and Lesser Ury.[7] In 1898 the Cassirer Art Salon opened in Berlin. Art dealer and publisher Paul Cassirer collaborated with his French colleague Paul Durand-Ruel to bring many of the most important works of French Impressionism to Berlin in quick succession, including Claude Monet's painting *Impression, Sunrise* (fig. 2) in 1899. With over 230 exhibitions of French and German artists, he kick-started the transfer of art. Ten exhibitions with works by Vincent van Gogh made the Dutch artist famous in Germany; his painting *Sunflowers* (1888, National Gallery, London) alone was shown four times at the art salon between 1901 and 1914. Édouard Manet's painting *The Luncheon on the Grass* (fig. 3) was also on view in Berlin in 1899, a year prior to the world exposition that would give Impressionism a gallery of its own for the first time. There, Manet's picture, which had hung in the Salon des Refusés in 1867, was showcased in a kind of honorary retrospective.

Display Window of Progress

Since the pre-March period, art had been viewed as one of three agents of progress: *la science, l'art,* and *l'industrie*. World expositions offered an arena for the international transfer of culture, where innovations from the increasingly differentiated natural sciences and fields of engineering could be presented along with the achievements of art. Although the French Impressionists were not included in the official program of a world's fair until 1900,[8] they were able to take advantage of the international mass audience by exhibiting in a pavilion of their own, like Manet in 1867, or mounting a major gallery exhibition, like Monet in 1889. Concurrently with the world exposition of 1889, the city of Paris celebrated the centennial of the French Revolution. Although German companies showed their products, the Kaiserreich refused to participate in the commemoration of the revolution and withdrew as an exhibitor. Three artists—Max Liebermann, along with Gotthardt Kuehl and Karl Köpping, who were living in Paris at the time—filled the vacuum and, at the invitation of the French organizer, formed an independent art section that was presented as part of the Décennale, an exhibition featuring art from the last ten years. In response, the German press accused them of a lack of patriotism.[9]

Max Liebermann had served as a medic during the war and went to Paris in 1873 shortly after the end of hostilities. The city was still under reconstruction from the damage caused by the suppression of the Paris Commune. Like the French Impressionists before him, Liebermann followed in the footsteps of the Barbizon painters and discovered plein-air painting. From then on, he repeatedly exhibited at the Paris Salon—for example, with his painting *Free Period in the Amsterdam Orphanage* (cat. 7) in 1882. For the unofficial German contribution to the world's fair of 1889, he chose Naturalist scenes or those painted *en plein air* by German artists such as Fritz von Uhde and Wilhelm Trübner, who broke with the official art of the empire.[10] Of the six works of his own that he selected, only the *Net Menders* (fig. 4) was new to the French public. French critic François Thiébault-Sisson highlighted the painting in his review,[11] and it was later acquired by Alfred Lichtwark for the collection of the Kunsthalle in Hamburg. The world exposition also brought Liebermann tremendous acclaim with the French public through a medal of honor and acceptance into the Société des Beaux-Arts. Despite Liebermann's efforts, imperial art policies would control the public image of German art for another fifteen years.

Against the backdrop of the economic boom of the late nineteenth century, participation in world expositions offered the new German Empire a forum

2
Claude Monet,
Impression, Sunrise, 1872,
Musée Marmottan Monet, Paris

3
Édouard Manet,
The Luncheon on the Grass, 1863,
Musée d'Orsay, Paris

for self-representation. In the sciences, Germany played a leading role with medical instruments such as the X-ray machine and with pioneering discoveries in the fields of organic chemistry, bacteriology, and optics. But as late as 1904, the excellence of the scientific avant-garde still stood in stark contrast to the manifestations of a regressive art policy. For the 1904 Louisiana Purchase Exposition, also known as the Saint Louis World's Fair, the emperor instructed Anton von Werner to select the artists.[12] The painters of the Berlin Secession were excluded, as were those of Germany's progressive art centers. With a reconstruction of Charlottenburg Palace for the German Pavilion, Wilhelm II also duped the federal parliamentary powers.[13] As the only national exhibition hall on the central plaza of the fairgrounds, the copy of the Prussian palace occupied a prominent place alongside the festival hall. On the interior, busts of the imperial family were displayed next to copies of Baroque paintings from the imperial collection. The Berlin satire magazine *Simplicissimus* caricatured it as the swan song of German art.[14]

4
Max Liebermann,
The Net Menders, 1887–89,
Hamburger Kunsthalle

Harry Graf Kessler, director of the Großherzogliches Museum (Grand Ducal Museum) in Weimar—which was planning the exhibition *Manet, Monet, Renoir, Cézanne* in 1904—criticized the imperial approach. Together with Liebermann as president of the Berlin Secession, he had founded a new artists' association in December 1903, the Deutscher Künstlerbund. In the accompanying magazine *Kunst und Künstler,* Kessler appealed to the Reichstag delegates.[15] He turned to the social-democratic, center, and progressive parties as well as to politicians from the national liberal and conservative parties, urging them to publicly discuss participation in world expositions and the allocation of funds. In the course of the debate, which took place on February 15–16, 1904, the government resolved to consider the interests of the Künstlerbund in the future, a decision that amounted to a removal of power from Anton von Werner. The headline in *The New York Times* read, "Kaiser, as Art Critic, Flouted in Reichstag."[16] Though a flop for the emperor, however, it was still not a victory for German Impressionism.

Shortly thereafter, Hugo von Tschudi, director of the Nationalgalerie in Berlin, was called upon to justify his purchases. In 1908 he fell into disfavor with the emperor for his acquisitions of works by Claude Monet, Alfred Sisley, and Paul Cézanne. Tschudi had made the purchases with the help of sponsors, and his dismissal thus also penalized private supporters. Anton von Werner took over the office of acting director, a setback for the avant-garde. The federal cultural system in Germany, however, made it possible for Tschudi to continue his support for French Impressionism at the Bayerische Staatsgemäldesammlungen (Bavarian State Painting Collections) in Munich.

The Battle for a New Art

The term *avant-garde* was adopted as a designation for utopian aesthetic approaches on the basis of its original military meaning (vanguard).[17] In this sense, it stands for the artistic manifestation of social, aesthetic, or political progress.[18] What is less often remembered is that in art criticism, the term was first applied to Impressionism as a battle cry of the middle-class elites.[19] French journalist Théodore Duret gave the title *Critique d'avant-garde* to his collection of Salon reports on Impressionism, written between 1870 and 1885 and pub-

lished in Paris in 1885 by Georges Charpentier, an early collector of Impressionist painting. Duret dedicated the volume to his friend Manet. Duret was a well-to-do Republican who represented his father's cognac business in Europe and made extended trips to the United States and Japan. He played a key role in the dissemination of Japanese woodcuts in France and the resulting rise of *Japonisme.* Manet first met him in 1865 during a journey to Spain and painted his portrait three years later (Musée des Beaux-Arts de la Ville de Paris). At the time, Duret still had reservations with regard to Impressionist painting, and it was not until the 1870s that he became an advocate and collector of Impressionist art.[20] In 1878 he published *Les Peintres impressionnistes* with chapters on Édouard Manet, Claude Monet, Berthe Morisot, Camille Pissarro, Pierre-Auguste Renoir, and Alfred Sisley. Duret also wrote monographs on Claude Monet (1880), James McNeill Whistler (1904)—who painted a portrait of Duret in 1883 (fig. 5)—Vincent Van Gogh (1916), and Pierre-Auguste Renoir (1924) and compiled the first catalogue raisonné of Manet's painting (1902). His prominence in the French art scene and that of his publishers Marguerite and Georges Charpentier, who hosted a salon and exhibitions in their editorial offices, suggests that the term *avant-garde* for Impressionism was already established and current in France since the publication of Duret's text (fig. 7).[21]

5
James McNeill Whistler,
Arrangement in Flesh Colour and Black: Portrait of Théodore Duret, 1883,
Metropolitan Museum of Art, New York

Duret described Monet's painterly approach and emphasized the inherent value of painting as such.[22] In so doing, he set in motion the most important aesthetic debate of the second half of the nineteenth century: that of the primacy of paint as a material and its autonomy with respect to the representation of the object. In his view, the Impressionists had emerged from the school of the Naturalists and followed Camille Corot, Gustave Courbet, and Manet.[23] In his book, the author identified himself with the role of the avant-gardist, whose texts would usher his readers into modernism. For him, the informal network of writers, publishers, and collectors that had formed around the Impressionists were as avant-garde as the artists themselves.[24] Duret also engaged in discussion of these themes with German artists such as Max Liebermann.

On April 15, 1901, Liebermann wrote to Duret asking for his help with a major Impressionist exhibition in Berlin. He inquired as to the possibility of borrowing a painting by Manet that belonged to Duret and asked him to arrange for the loan of another work by the same artist from a French private collection. The tone of the letter was friendly and familiar; the concern was to help Impressionism achieve a breakthrough.[25] The shared goal was an artistic one. But in 1908, in the midst of the conflict with the emperor, Liebermann wrote to Duret for political reasons. He asked him to advocate for Tschudi in France in order to create pressure from abroad against the latter's dismissal.[26] Duret was not unknown in Germany: in 1904, his article "Claude Monet und der Impressionismus" (Claude Monet and Impressionism) had appeared in the magazine *Kunst und Künstler,*[27] and in 1909 his book *Die Impressionisten* (The Impressionists) was issued by Bruno Cassirer, who had established the publishing house Bruno & Paul Cassirer Kunst- und Verlagsanstalt in Berlin in 1898 with his cousin Paul Cassirer. Together they edited the magazine *Kunst und Künstler* and published the letters of Van Gogh along with writings by Lovis Corinth; Max Liebermann; Alfred Lichtwark, the director of the Hamburg Kunsthalle; and philosopher Ernst Cassirer, as well as Hermann Cohen's edition of Kant. Just as it made sense to exhibit Max Liebermann alongside Edgar Degas in the gallery program of the art salon in 1898, so it seemed self-evident to publish Duret's book alongside Liebermann's *Die Phantasie in der Malerei* (Imagination in Painting, 1903)—if somewhat belatedly, since the first French edition had appeared almost forty years before. As late as 1909, while still fighting to gain acceptance for the Impressionists in France, Duret gave the Germans astonishingly high marks for their reception of Manet. That year the art magazine *Cicerone* noted with regard to Duret's foreword to the catalog of an Impressionist exhibition at Galerie Bernheim-Jeune in Paris, "Duret writes quite flatteringly about us Germans: 'Today, Manet holds a higher place in the general opinion in Germany than he has been able to conquer in France. . . . It is the Germans who were the first to see rightly and who, by seeing rightly, first put Manet's art in its true place.'"[28]

In the rapidly growing cities of Germany, a wide range of gallery exhibitions, the professionalization of the museums, scientific progress, and developments in the educational system fueled interest in an art that had less to do with national culture than with modern civilization, an art that was rational and future-oriented and gave expression to the individual. Art magazines such as *Pan* (1895) and *Kunst und Künstler* (1902), the collections of the mercantile middle class, and purchases by museums in Germany led to the internationalization of Impressionism. The acceptance of German art by French art critics and the important acquisition of Max Liebermann's painting *Beer Garden in Brannenburg* by the Musée du Luxembourg in 1894 (cat. 28) also contributed to this development.[29] At exhibitions in their pavilion on the Kurfürstendamm in the heart of Berlin, the Berlin Secession showed not only the artists of Naturalism but also Impressionists such as Fritz von Uhde, Maria Slavona, and Max Slevogt.

Since the 1880s, art critics in France who, like Edmond Duranty, supported the Impressionists (fig. 6) had invoked a common European spirit. Duranty was a leader in this movement. In 1876 he had given the title *La Nouvelle Peinture* to his review of the second Impressionist exhibition: the new art was European. In reviews of the contributions of German artists to the world expositions in Paris, Duranty expressed optimism that the culture war among the great modern nations was unnecessary.[30] In Germany after 1900, a similar informal network championed Impressionism as a *new* art. In addition to museum directors such as Harry Graf Kessler, Alfred Lichtwark, Gustav Pauli, and Hugo von Tschudi, who promoted their purchases in the new art magazines and devoted monographs to Impressionism,[31] art critics and connoisseurs of the French scene such as Julius Elias, Julius Meier-Graefe, Richard Muther, Karl Scheffler, and Hermann Uhde-Bernays also emerged as protagonists in Germany—and were subjected to accusations of unpatriotic behavior.[32] Among them, Emil Heilbut enjoyed the closest contact with the French avant-garde.[33]

Under the pseudonym Herman(n) Helferich, Heilbut began writing exhibition reviews for liberal magazines such as *Die Nation* and the art journal *Die Kunst für Alle* in the 1880s. In 1887 he published a collection of his articles from *Die Nation* under the title *Neue Kunst* (New Art), an allusion to Duranty's *La Nouvelle Peinture.* This reference to the avant-garde discourse in France was not an isolated instance. In 1887 he published his *Studie über den Naturalismus*

6
Edgar Degas,
Portrait of Edmond Duranty, 1879,
Burrel Collection, Glasgow

7
Pierre-Auguste Renoir,
Madame Georges Charpentier and Her Children, Georgette-Berthe and Paul-Émile-Charles, 1878,
Metropolitan Museum of Art, New York

und Max Liebermann (Study on Naturalism and Max Liebermann).[34] In it, he ascribed a certain "intransigence" to Liebermann,[35] and in so doing echoed an early self-designation of the group around Monet, who had called themselves "the Intransigents."[36] Heilbut applied the description to Liebermann, along with other militant qualities. According to him, Liebermann was an "agent provocateur,"[37] "the most outstanding of the German Naturalists, unconstrained, unleashed, never slick and entrapped, as all, all of the others seem to quietly, continually, gradually become. He does not grow tame."[38]

Heilbut characterized Liebermann's Naturalism as a "new art," once again alluding to Duranty's text. "But we believe that it is this art, if any, that belongs to the future. It tills virgin soil, its territory is the only one in which its predecessors left something to do . . . then there will be a general recognition that the new art is also the better art."[39] With these words, Heilbut struck a new chord in art criticism.[40] Like Duret, he made himself an apologist for the avant-garde and advocated for its new worldliness.[41] Heilbut derived avant-garde potential from the Naturalism of Liebermann, whom he saw as a forerunner of Impressionism.[42] Liebermann, in turn, expressed enthusiasm over Heilbut and valued his opinion.[43]

8
Claude Monet,
Road at La Cavée in Pourville, 1882,
private collection

For the next phase of his campaign, Heilbut used his collection of works by Claude Monet, which with four paintings was the largest in Germany (figs. 8, 9).[44] In 1889, only a few years after their creation, he displayed three of them during his lecture on Monet at the Großherzogliche Kunstschule (Grand Ducal Art School) in Weimar. They were the first paintings by Monet to be shown in Germany after the exhibition of the collection of Felicie and Carl Bernstein, which had taken place at Galerie Gurlitt in Berlin in 1883. The following year, Heilbut published the first German-language text on the artist.[45] Finally, Bruno Cassirer's founding of the magazine *Kunst und Künstler* in 1902 made it possible for Heilbut to bring his influence to bear as editor-in-chief. Returning to the writings of the French avant-garde, he now concentrated on Émile Zola, whose Salon reviews he published in German along with Zola's text on Manet.[46] In a letter to Heilbut from the spring of 1903, Max Liebermann commented:

> *I think it was quite right for you to translate* Mes Haines. *Zola's criticism is especially relevant for Germany now: we are hobbling along a generation behind; but I am also convinced that Impressionism—the final goal of painting—which is almost pronounced dead in its native land, will awaken to new life here. And just as you made yourself the spokesman for Naturalism twenty years ago with your earliest criticism, so now you will become the champion of Impressionism. To be sure, Impressionism is only a catchword; what I mean by it is good painting, made for its own sake, cured of any purpose.*[47]

Heilbut's campaign and the diverse initiatives of the informal network resulted in change from 1904 on. After the debate in the Reichstag and Tschudi's dismissal, a new openness to painting "for its own sake" arose, which at times even mitigated the still-prevailing chauvinism: while previous reviewers of Secessionist exhibitions had avoided comparing Liebermann and other German artists to the French Impressionists out of anti-French sentiment, such comparisons were now viewed as a distinction. Even Caspar David Friedrich was celebrated as a precursor of Impressionism during his rediscovery at the centennial exhibition of 1906.[48] Impressionism had fulfilled its role as the first avant-garde and was already being put forward as a standard for the canon of modern painting. In the conflict over the purchase of Van Gogh's *Field with Poppies* (1889, Kunsthalle Bremen) for the Kunsthalle Bremen in 1911, national boundaries were once again invoked—this time by artists, who felt disadvantaged and overlooked.[49] But a new development was already making itself felt: among the supporters of an international acquisition policy for Germany were Max Beckmann and Wassily Kandinsky, painters who would lead the way from Impressionism to Expressionism.

Translated from German by Melissa M. Thorson

9
Claude Monet,
Boat on the Seine at Jeufosse, 1884,
private collection

Max Liebermann

The Reception of French Impressionism in the German Kaiserreich

Barbara Schaefer

In France in the late 1860s and 1870s, the Impressionists—as they were later called—developed an artistic approach that vehemently rejected time-honored traditions of European art. They refused the notion that high art should devote itself exclusively to lofty historical, mythological, or biblical themes and instead focused their attention on contemporary people, places, and events. They wanted to evoke impressions of the natural world around them, momentary snapshots of the movement of water or clouds, the fleeting qualities of light, the ever-changing appearance of reflected luminosity on natural forms. They captured their unmistakable views on the canvas with loose, energetic brushstrokes, bright hues, and colored shadows (fig. 1), infusing their perceptions of atmospheric moods with an extraordinary sense of spontaneity. When these artists debuted in public at their first independent exhibition in 1874, the critics accordingly dubbed them "Impressionists,"[1] a name they proudly adopted for themselves shortly thereafter.

At first, contemporary viewers perceived the paintings as crude and sketch-like, at odds with the habits of seeing that the official art world—in other words, the Salon exhibitions—had inculcated in them. Preference was given to works that adhered to academic principles, that embraced serious pictorial themes and showcased the traditional artistic skills of drawing and modeling.

In protest over their repeated rejection by the Salon, the Impressionists-to-be founded the Société Anonyme des Artistes Peintres, Sculpteurs, Graveurs, etc. (Anonymous Society of Painters, Sculptors, Engravers, etc.), which organized eight independent exhibitions between 1874 and 1886. In this way they not only succeeded in developing innovative painterly techniques and elevating modern motifs to picture-worthy status but also liberated themselves from the constraints of the official art establishment of the day.

Early Modern Art in Berlin

By the time the last of these exhibitions was on view in Paris in 1886, the heyday of French Impressionism had passed and the transition to Post-Impressionism and Symbolism as the newest forms of modern artistic expression was already underway. Much of what had scandalized visitors to the first exhibition on the Boulevard des Capucines in 1874 now enjoyed popularity with influential art critics, dealers, and collectors. Among the latter were Carl and Felicie Bernstein, who brought paintings by Édouard Manet, Claude Monet, Camille Pissarro, Alfred Sisley, and others from Paris to Berlin in 1882. The Bernsteins were the first collectors of French Impressionist painting in Germany, and their top-tier holdings included such masterpieces as Manet's *The Folkestone Boat, Boulogne* (fig. 2) and *White Lilacs* (fig. 3).

In October 1883 the first exhibition of French Impressionism in Germany opened at Galerie Fritz Gurlitt in Berlin,[2] with a selection of works that included ten paintings from the Bernstein collection. In the press, the exhibited works were harshly criticized for their sketch-like quality and lack of technical skill:

> *The landscape painters seek out the most uninteresting areas and render them with as few colors as possible in the most trite and trivial way. They place one patch of color next to another . . . and do not trouble themselves in the least to further model the forms. . . . They have a special fondness for the crudest colors . . . and anxiously seek to avoid all that might please the eye. At the exhibition at Gurlitt's . . . the best-known proponents of this primitive conception of nature are represented.*[3]

1
Alfred Sisley,
Snow Effect in Louveciennes, 1874,
Hasso Plattner Collection,
Museum Barberini, Potsdam

2
Édouard Manet,
The Folkestone Boat, Boulogne, ca. 1868–72,
Philadelphia Museum of Art

At that time, the salon of the Bernsteins also served as an exhibition forum—a gathering place for guests from the world of science and art—even if the privilege of inspecting the works in their private collection was available only to a relatively small circle of art lovers. Among the latter was Max Liebermann: "What interested me the most were the Impressionist paintings the Bernsteins had acquired through their cousin Charles Ephrussi."[4] The Bernsteins thus played an important role in the reception of Impressionism in Germany from the mid-1880s on, although their collection was certainly not without its detractors.[5] Indeed, it would not be until the following decade, starting in the mid-1890s, that the influence of French Impressionism on younger German painters would become perceptible. This fact, and the reasons for this approximately twenty-year delay in the deliberate reception of French Impressionism in the painting of the German Kaiserreich, are the subject of this essay.[6]

Max Liebermann in Paris

A determinative factor in this regard was the Franco-Prussian War of 1870–71—or rather, the tense political relationship between the two countries that dominated the postwar period and fundamentally impeded ongoing artistic exchange.[7] After the founding of the German Reich under Emperor Wilhelm I in 1871, the aspiration arose for Germany to distinguish itself among the peoples—and differentiate itself from them—through a national art. Even after 1888, under Wilhelm II, the grandson of Wilhelm I, the official Wilhelmine art establishment concentrated on an academic Historicism that devoted itself to historical and mythological themes. The conservative, idealistic aesthetic of the imperial court in Berlin was to have a lasting effect on art and sculpture in Germany; painterly innovations tended to alienate audiences. Given the political circumstances of the preceding war, these prejudices were aimed in particular at Impressionism from France, and motifs such as pure landscape—as well as the scenes from everyday reality favored by young, progressive artists—were rejected as unworthy subjects for painting.[8]

Notwithstanding the political tension, after his training in Weimar between 1868 and 1872, Liebermann moved to Paris. While finishing his studies there between 1873 and 1878, he regularly spent the summers in Holland, and even in Paris it was the Dutch Old Masters he studied in the Louvre that strongly influenced him, rather than, remarkably, the Impressionism that was currently on the rise. Like his fellow artist and countryman Wilhelm Leibl, Liebermann was enthusiastic about Frans Hals, and his time in Paris was also marked by a renewed interest in the oeuvre of Mihály Munkácsy, who had lived there since 1872 and had previously inspired him during an encounter in Düsseldorf. However, the narrative frequently repeated in art-historical writing—that Liebermann took no notice of contemporaneous Impressionism during his time in Paris and became familiar with it only later in 1883, at the home of the Bernsteins—is refuted by a later interview: "Manet remains the still point of his [that is, Liebermann's] art world. It is forever a shame that the two great Impressionists never came into personal contact with each other! Liebermann tells how happened: once—it was shortly after the Seventies Wars [Franco-Prussian War] in Paris, when a mutual acquaintance suggested to Manet that he introduce Liebermann to him, the Frenchman declined."[9] It would also have been strange if Liebermann had not come across the innovations of Impressionism during his extended sojourn in Paris, especially since the first three Impressionist exhibitions, which caused quite a stir in the art world, took place there in 1874, 1876, and 1877. The conclusive evidence, however, was presented by Liebermann himself in an 1896 essay in the art magazine *Pan:* ". . . and I confess that when I saw the first paintings of the Impressionists thirty years ago, I couldn't make heads or tails of them. One has to learn to see, just as one has to learn to hear a movement by Beethoven."[10] Thus by his own admission, Liebermann did not immediately resonate with the atmospheric quality of French Impressionism; yet at the same time, it is also quite possible that "an artistic approach rejected by the broad public . . . [had to] seem unsuited to the professional advancement of an aspiring artist whose highest goal was recognition."[11]

3
Édouard Manet,
White Lilacs, ca. 1882,
Alte Nationalgalerie, Berlin

The Development of Modernism in Germany in the 1880s

In the 1880s, an interest in Impressionism—in the liberation of color and the phenomenon of light—increasingly took hold among younger artists in Germany. At this point, however, the resulting artistic conception could by no means be described as Impressionist. For while countless artists adopted a brighter palette in order to bring light into their pictures, one searches in vain for the dissolution of contour and detail. Instead, the manifestations of this *Hellmalerei* (bright painting) are quite heterogeneous, differing not least of all according to region.

At that time, Munich—which was far from the capital of the Reich and thus far from the direct influence of the imperial court—gained considerable importance as a location for exhibitions, but also for education. It was there that teachers such as Wilhelm von Diez, Ludwig von Löfftz, and Wilhelm von Lindenschmit the Younger exposed their students not only to more recent Dutch painting, which at the time was already admired, but also—in initial steps—to a modern French direction.[12] Subsequently, other academies in Germany would likewise devote increasing attention to the modern tendencies emerging on all sides that showed an affinity with Impressionism. Teachers such as Heinrich von Zügel (fig. 6), who came to Munich in 1895—as well as Gotthardt Kuehl, who was active in Dresden from 1895 on (fig. 5), and Wilhelm Trübner, who taught in Frankfurt am Main after 1896—may be described as painters who employed the stylistic means of Impressionism. Furthermore, beyond the walls of the academy, progressive private art schools—such as that of Slovenian painter Anton Ažbe in Munich, probably the best known of them today—encouraged a stylistic development that "led from a refined, picturesque Realism to plein-air painting and finally to an Impressionist conception."[13] A new tenor was also perceptible in the work of Liebermann, who moved from Paris to Munich in 1878, or of Fritz von Uhde, or also of Lovis Corinth, who spent time in Munich in the 1880s. The latter, however, were not yet directly indebted to French Impressionism, but in many cases were still emulating the French plein-air painters of Barbizon from the 1830s and 1840s, as well as, not least of all, the *alla prima* painting of Leibl (fig. 4).[14]

4
Wilhelm Leibl,
Reindl the Veterinarian in the Arbor, ca. 1890,
Städtische Galerie im Lenbachhaus und Kunstbau, Munich

A significant artistic event that marked the close of the 1880s was the 1889 Exposition Universelle in Paris. Although Chancellor Otto von Bismarck had refused any German participation in the exposition since it was intended to commemorate the centennial of the French Revolution and laud the realization of its ideals, Liebermann nonetheless succeeded in organizing an exhibition of work by German artists. This act of self-distancing from the paternalism of the imperial art establishment followed the emancipatory model of France, and from then on Liebermann was viewed there as the leading representative of modern German art. In Germany, too, he subsequently emerged as probably the most important but also the most controversial artist of his day. That same year, in 1889, the first painting by Liebermann entered the collection of a German museum when the artist gave *The Flax Barn at Laren* from 1887 (fig. p. 268) to the Nationalgalerie in Berlin. Purchases by other important museums soon followed: in 1889, the *Net Menders* (fig. p. 24) was donated to the Hamburger Kunsthalle, and in 1891 the painting *Woman with Goats in the Dunes* (1891) was acquired from the artist by the Pinakothek in Munich, sealing Liebermann's official recognition. *Beer Garden in Brannenburg* of 1893 (cat. 28) may serve as an example of Liebermann's work from the 1890s: the sunlight filtering onto the scene is rendered in bright, impasto patches, the view of nature now acquires greater significance, and the atmospheric effect is more strongly emphasized. As has been observed, paintings like this suggest that although the encounter with Impressionism at the Bernsteins' was not Liebermann's first exposure to the movement, it was there that he "learned to see it" and "now grasped it in its full significance."[15]

Germany in the 1890s: Modern Exhibition Practice

The year 1890 saw the first exhibition in Germany in which works by French Impressionists were made accessible to a broader public. The show, which took place in Weimar, introduced a new form of landscape painting, with works by Claude Monet, Alfred Sisley, Camille Pissarro, and Edgar Degas. Remarkably, the exhibition was organized by the academy in Weimar, which had been founded only relatively recently in 1860.[16] Almost immediately, so-called Secessionist movements initiated modern efforts to resist the dominant exhibition policies of dusty academicism. The first artists' association that sought to create an independent forum for the exhibition of their (diverging) artistic innovations was founded in Munich in April 1892. Other Secessionist groups followed their example, including the Berlin Secession under the leadership of Liebermann, which opened its first exhibition on May 19, 1899. The official, state-sponsored art establishment in Berlin adopted a critical stance toward the new organization, and the emperor's disapproval was widely known. The fact, moreover, that a number of Jewish public figures, including Liebermann, had played a leading role in the founding of the Secession also gave rise to hostility.

The Berlin Secession was headed by Liebermann until 1911; during the same period, he was also president of the Deutscher Künstlerbund,[17] holding positions that were opposed to the emperor's conservative views.[18] Despite all his efforts to avoid political and religious confrontation, Liebermann's advocacy for modern French art put him at the center of controversies and politicized his activities in various and complex ways.[19] It became his declared goal to show examples of modern French art again and again—works he considered suitable to replace academic traditions. The regular inclusion of French Impressionist works in exhibitions of art by contemporary German artists also served to buttress the significance of Impressionism as the origin of the modern direction. This exhibition practice took root and would continue until the outbreak of World War I, ultimately contributing decisively to the spread of French Impressionism throughout all of German-speaking Europe. In 1903 the Vienna Secession (founded in 1897) presented their important Sixteenth Exhibition under the title *Entwicklung des Impressionismus in Malerei und Plastik* (Development of Impressionism in Painting and Sculpture). In addition to a section entitled "Anfänge und Entwicklung" (Beginnings and Development), it predominantly featured works by the *peintres impressionnistes* from France, including Manet's portrait of *Eva Gonzalès* (1870, National Gallery, London) and his painting *A Bar at the Folies-Bergère* (1882, Courtauld Institute, London). The exhibition also highlighted the "Übergänge zum Stil" (Transitions to the Style), presenting artists such as Vincent van Gogh and Paul Gauguin as direct forerunners of the then-contemporary artistic approach.[20]

5
Gotthardt Kuehl,
The Garden Room, 1895–1900,
Albertinum, Dresden

Impressionism Has the Floor: Collectors, Museums, the Art Market, and Art Criticism after 1900

Many of the works in such exhibitions were made available by Berlin art dealer Paul Cassirer, who in turn cultivated close connections with his Paris colleague Paul Durand-Ruel. Cassirer began as secretary and became a board member of the Berlin Secession in 1912. He played a key role as a procurer of foreign art, and his clientele included major private collectors in Germany as well as numerous galleries. Ultimately, however, he was only reacting to the demand that emerged with the gradual acceptance of Impressionism in Germany. To be sure, this development also resulted in an unexpected increase in prices, which maneuvered the directors of public collections into the sidelines.

Private collectors—often bankers, entrepreneurs, or physicians—who had no need to defend their purchases before a commission and had sufficient financial means to purchase top-tier pieces were not subject to these constraints.[21] Among the ranks of contemporary artists, Liebermann was the only one to amass a comparably high-quality collection of modern French art.[22] In 1896, moreover—shortly after Hugo von Tschudi took office as director of the Nationalgalerie in Berlin—it was Liebermann who traveled with him to Paris to examine works by French Impressionists at the gallery of Durand-Ruel.

Tschudi immediately recognized their significance and the need to familiarize museumgoers in Berlin with French Impressionism, "in order to understand the development of contemporary German art."[23]

Without delay, Tschudi integrated nineteenth-century landscape painting into the hanging of the Nationalgalerie in Berlin as the dominant genre—from the English landscapists of the early nineteenth century and the Barbizon painters to the French Impressionists—a move that elicited massive criticism. His presentation gave precedence to "purely painterly" forms of expression over "serious" pictorial content, alienating the adherents of an idealistic art. Furthermore, viewers with nationalistic sentiments were incensed by the presentation of German art as directly dependent on French models. Emperor Wilhelm II,[24] who at that time was still the leading voice in the German art establishment, became Tschudi's most influential adversary. In his oft-quoted 1901 speech on "gutter art," the emperor asserted:

> *Art that violates the laws and goes beyond the bounds I have indicated is no longer art.... Art should assist in educating the public. By way of its ideals, it should also offer [the members of] the lower classes the opportunity—after a day of strenuous work and effort—to refresh and strengthen themselves.... If art, now, does no more than portray misery—as it happens so often today—in an even more dreadful light than that in which it is already cast, then it sins against the German people.... And if culture is to fully fulfill its duty, it must penetrate the lowest levels of society. Art can only do this [however] when it offers its hand, when it elevates, when it does not lower itself into the gutter instead.*[25]

Ultimately, Tschudi's vehement support of French modernism would lead to his dismissal as director of the Nationalgalerie in Berlin in 1909. From there he went to Munich, where he took over leadership of the Bavarian State Painting Collections, which in turn contributed to the modernization of Munich's museums.[26]

By now, the "victory march" of French Impressionism in Germany could no longer be halted. The gallery of Paul and Bruno Cassirer presented (sales) exhibitions of works by French Impressionists in quick succession. Other galleries followed suit, and from the turn of the century onward, "modern" artists in Germany increasingly recognized the exemplary character of French Impressionism. This process was reinforced by the progressive art magazine *Kunst und Künstler* (Art and Artists) published by Bruno Cassirer: under the editorship of Karl Scheffler, it was understood as a mouthpiece of Impressionism and was responsible for the spread of modernist conceptions of art in German-speaking Europe. The period around and after the year 1900 thus saw the development of a cross-pollinating constellation of art dealers, wealthy collectors, art historians, and exhibition-makers that helped French Impressionism achieve its breakthrough in the German Kaiserreich. Art critics and art writers too increasingly turned their attention to Impressionism. Adherents of idealistic conceptions claimed that it lacked depth of feeling, while nationalistically minded critics rejected the "adoption of such French fashions," which, they said, had hitherto "been of more harm than use to Germans."[27] To some extent, this criticism anticipated the 1911 publication of *Ein Protest Deutscher Künstler* (A Protest of German Artists),[28] which, in response to the purchase of Vincent van Gogh's *Field with Poppies* (1889) by the Kunsthalle in Bremen, denounced the alleged infiltration of German art by foreign, especially French influences, an accusation that was accompanied by obvious antisemitic tendencies. Progressive art writers, on the other hand, acknowledged French Impressionism as the most important foundation for a modern art that was continuing to develop into the present. In 1904 Julius Meier-Graefe, then living in Paris, published his highly influential *Entwicklungsgeschichte der modernen Kunst* (Developmental History of Modern Art).[29] Focusing on the art of the nineteenth century, Meier-Graefe gave primacy to the artistic principle of the "purely painterly." He identified a clear line of development from Peter Paul Rubens and Diego Velázquez through Eugène Delacroix and Honoré Daumier to thc "four pillars of modern painting":[30] Édouard Manet, Paul Cézanne, Edgar Degas, and Pierre-Auguste Renoir.[31] His positions would be determinative for the ongoing development of artistic taste in Germany, and thus also defined the subsequent reception of Impressionism in German-speaking Europe. There, in the ensuing years, Impressionism would be considered *the* pioneering artistic style of the late nineteenth century; France was the point of reference. To be sure, the outbreak of World War I in 1914 marked a caesura, and with the war and its aftermath the bond between France and Germany was once again torn asunder—along with the exchange between modern artists.

6
Heinrich von Zügel,
Boy with Steer, 1896,
Alte Nationalgalerie, Berlin

Coda

As a painter and private art collector in Wilhelmine Germany, Max Liebermann frequently stood in the line of fire. Not only did he play a key role in the development of modern art during that period; he also served as a link between the modern art scene in Germany and the German-Jewish elite who supported progress and change. His prominence in the public eye exposed him and his circle to an antisemitism that was increasingly associated with antimodern sensibilities. Ultimately, Liebermann's life and work exemplify the extent to which identification with modernism reinforced the perception of Jews as outsiders in Wilhelmine society. Liebermann was independent and loyal to his Jewish roots but also wanted to be accepted and respected by imperial society. Moreover, as a German artist he demanded artistic autonomy, and as a member of the liberal bourgeoisie he asserted the right to personal freedom, to support the German and French avant-garde without fear of reprisal.[32]

In his own oeuvre, Liebermann decided to work within the mainstream of the modernist repertoire of motifs, with his early phase strongly influenced by Realism. Dutch art was also enormously influential; as late as 1897, he wrote to German collector Max Linde from Laren in Holland: "But there is only one country in the world for painting, c'est la Hollande."[33] His interest in Judaism and Jewish themes, in turn, left its mark in his numerous studies of the Jewish quarter in Amsterdam (cat. 12). He turned his attention more and more to contemporary everyday life, just as the French Impressionists had done. Like his French colleagues, Liebermann increasingly propounded the view that the pictorial interpretation of modern life was the task of the modern artist.

As a patron, Max Liebermann began collecting French Impressionism in the 1890s, an activity that influenced his own work both in terms of style and subject matter, and also began to employ a brighter palette. After the turn of the century, Liebermann increasingly accepted portrait commissions from the middle and educated class in Germany, a circle that included politicians, writers, and luminaries. All of these portraits are executed in a somewhat minimalistic style. Ultimately, however, it would be Liebermann's beach and riding scenes, his images of beer gardens (fig. 7), holiday resorts, country houses, and landscapes, and most of all his later paintings of the Wannsee that would earn him a reputation as one of the leading German Impressionists. As Liebermann stated on the occasion of the tenth anniversary of the Berlin Secession: "The founding of the Secession . . . coincides with the increasing triumph of Impressionism. But Impressionism is not—as one daily hears or reads—a direction, but rather a worldview: everyone can, in accord with his talent, be blessed by it."[34]

Translated from German by Melissa M. Thorson

7
Max Liebermann,
Beer Garden in Munich, 1884,
Neue Pinakothek, Munich

Alexander Bastek

Everyday Narratives

Genre Painting in German Impressionism

In 1874, when a group of modern French painters—among them Paul Cézanne, Edgar Degas, Claude Monet, Berthe Morisot, Camille Pissarro, Pierre-Auguste Renoir, and Alfred Sisley—mounted their first independent exhibition at the former studio of photographer Gaspard-Félix Tournachon, known as Nadar, on the Boulevard des Capucines, Max Liebermann was also in Paris. In his review, art critic Louis Leroy described the show as an "exhibition of the Impressionists," based on the title of Claude Monet's painting *Impression, Sunrise* (fig. p. 23).[1] During the birth of French Impressionism, Liebermann was studying seventeenth-century Dutch painters in the Louvre and exhibiting his *Women Plucking Geese* (1871–72, Alte Nationalgalerie, Berlin) at the Paris Salon.

Framing his review as a fictitious gallery conversation with Joseph Vincent, an invented landscape painter,[2] Leroy accused the Impressionists of disregarding traditional artistic form and convention. For him, mere "impression" meant the abandonment of content and pictorial narrative. Although at that time Liebermann was still far from being an Impressionist painter—he had not yet brightened his palette—like modern French artists he too broke with the convention of depicting historical, religious, or edifying themes in narrative form. In *Women Plucking Geese,* he presented an image that showed not a story, but a sequence of labor. While contemporary critics praised the veracity of the picture, they also decried the mere plucking of feathers as a motif unworthy of painting. In his "Studie über den Naturalismus und Max Liebermann" (Study on Naturalism and Max Liebermann) from 1887, art critic Emil Heilbut maintained that the offense caused by the theme of women plucking geese resulted from the expectation of a "historical tragedy" for an artist's debut work.[3] A painting such as Carl Theodor von Piloty's *Seni at the Dead Body of Wallenstein* (1855, Neue Pinakothek, Munich) exemplifies this kind of historical tragedy with its portrayal of a famous and comprehensible story from the Thirty Years' War. Piloty, moreover, showed a moment that prompted viewers to remember what had previously transpired and look ahead to what might follow—the "fruitful moment" championed by Gotthold Ephraim Lessing.[4] In comparison, the moments captured by modern artists seemed, as it were, fruitless. Heilbut thus also articulated the distinction between

Liebermann's Naturalist scenes of everyday life and the popular genre pictures of the day, whose everyday scenes were quite familiar to the public. According to Heilbut, Liebermann's works differed from the latter in their lack of easily understandable anecdotal content; in his view, what Liebermann wanted to offer was not "laughing or weeping dramas," not comedies or tragedies, but painting.[5] Nevertheless, in *Women Plucking Geese* Liebermann still adhered to a compositional scheme typical of genre painting, the "peephole view" in which the pictorial space opens up toward the viewer in theater-like fashion, with a slightly elevated (stage) floor and a backdrop positioned parallel to the picture plane. In so doing, he adopted an approach suitable for staging figures, connecting them in storylines, and guiding the viewer's eye through the picture along a narrative path.

Liebermann used his sojourn in Paris as an opportunity to make regular trips to the Netherlands. In addition to his study of the Old Masters, his pictorial motifs were increasingly informed by the landscape and people of Holland. In 1889 the artist recalled, "Around this time, I began painting pictures from nature or at least starting them in front of nature, a principle to which I have remained faithful to this day."[6]

The 1885 painting *Street in a Dutch Village* (fig. 1) shows that in Liebermann's hands, motifs observed from everyday life could still carry classical narrative potential. The painting is said to have been based on a sketch the artist brought back from his honeymoon in 1884, when he visited Laren, among other places.[7] Perhaps the simplest point of departure for a narrative is an encounter between persons: in Liebermann's painting, two peasant girls meet while passing on the street in opposite directions, pausing to look at each other and probably engaging in a brief conversation. The viewer's gaze follows the narrative from motif to motif along the winding, slightly ascending lane. Liebermann sprinkled numerous smaller episodes both on and beside the path. The 1994 gallery handbook of the state museum of Lower Saxony formulates the following story:

1
Max Liebermann,
Street in a Dutch Village, 1885,
Niedersächsisches Landesmuseum Hannover

> *Along the street, still wet from the last rain, trudges a cow. In front of it is a horse-drawn wagon, on which a tired laborer seems to have just fallen asleep. A small dog excitedly follows his young master, tail held high. At the same time, a farmer in wooden shoes crosses the street from the right. And once again it is the bearing of each figure, no matter how small, that Liebermann emphasizes. This man (like all the other persons in the picture) shows that despite his bustling activity, he still has plenty of time. One hand is shoved into the pocket of his trousers. And for the artist, even a strutting rooster along with other poultry is a worthy anecdotal enrichment to the far right foreground.*[8]

This genre painting, however (or *Sittenbild,* "picture reflecting customs and manners," as it was described in an exhibition review of 1888[9]), marks the end of a phase of anecdotal, narrative pictures and points the way to a new phase of open landscapes.[10] Probably the best-known work from this transitional period, *The Net Menders* (fig. p. 24), was also painted from sketches the artist brought back from his honeymoon. Liebermann's portrayal of figures working in the open air straddles the boundary between landscape and genre, while the large scale of the piece places it in the tradition of history painting. His pictorial theme, however, is the rhythmic arrangement of figures within the deep space of the landscape, achieved by depicting the various activities involved in mending the nets. The large figure in the foreground, pensively gazing into the distance, introduces a reflective dimension to the image.[11] This reflectiveness, in turn, suggests the beginning of a possible narrative that could be derived from the genre scene.

Orphanage Scenes: Visual Narratives of the Bourgeoisie

At the Paris World's Fair in 1889, Max Liebermann had organized an exhibition of contemporary German art together with Lübeck artist Gotthardt Kuehl. In a letter to Kuehl, Liebermann remarked the following with regard to this "private" showing of German painting (since there was no official German participation in the exposition):[12] "Incidentally, I think the Paris exhibition will also help our view prevail in Germany, and that the brown Munich gravy—the locals here don't even have that—will be cleaned up once and for all."[13] As far as the advancement of modern painting was concerned, therefore, Liebermann and Kuehl shared the same point of view.[14]

Kuehl had lived in Paris since 1879, and, like Liebermann, also visited the Netherlands on multiple occasions. At the Salon of 1882, moreover, he was also able to see Liebermann's *Free Period in the Amsterdam Orphanage* (cat. 7) from a year earlier, which probably inspired him to adopt the same pictorial motif. The painting by Liebermann brings together multiple figures in larger and smaller groups, involved in various encounters and activities such as sewing. The patches of light on the ground, however, call attention to an empty area that violates every convention for introducing the viewer's eye to a visual story: the spots of sunlight point to nothing but a few leaves and some pecking birds. In a study for this painting created in 1876, *Courtyard of the Orphanage in Amsterdam* (Arp Museum Bahnhof Rolandseck, Remagen), the empty space is even more extensive and leads along the visual axis to an open doorway in the background. Here, the eye no longer finds any discernable narrative thread as it wanders through the picture.

In his study-like painting *The Dutch Sewing School* of 1876 (fig. 3), Liebermann shows the orphan girls seated on benches in an interior. The side view of the hall brings the clearly ordered rows of benches into a dynamic diagonal structure. Here, the pictorial narrative of earlier works is superseded by a more painterly aspect, a rhythmic arrangement that leads our gaze leftward and into pictorial depth, following a meandering path through the rows of benches and along the light-colored bonnets and collars of the orphan girls.

Kuehl found models for his orphanage paintings in his home city of Lübeck. The first of these works (cat. 9) was completed in Paris in 1884[15] and was exhibited at the Salon the same year. Here the artist seems to be depicting a scene he had observed on the upper floor of the orphanage in Lübeck. Four girls in red dresses and blue aprons sit on wooden benches, sewing. Three of them look down, concentrating on their work; the second girl from the right, however, lifts her head and gazes at the viewer. Kuehl thus adopts a compositional strategy to draw us into the image, a subject to which we will return later. He also uses painterly means as well as positioning to further

2
Gotthardt Kuehl,
In the Lübeck Orphanage (Triptych), ca. 1895,
Albertinum, Dresden

3
Max Liebermann,
The Dutch Sewing School, 1876,
Von der Heydt-Museum Wuppertal

emphasize the girl's special role. The fabric she sews is not white, but red, and she is seated slightly higher than the other figures with a checkered cloth over her shoulders. With the fallen bench in the foreground, Kuehl introduces an element that will frequently recur in his paintings: an arranged, seemingly random detail that suggests he observed the scene in exactly this way—an orchestrated impression, one might say.

4
Max Liebermann,
Tennis Players by the Sea (First Version), 1901,
Museum Kunst der Westküste, Alkersum/Föhr

The extent to which Kuehl's paintings were carefully staged and composed is demonstrated by his 1895 triptych *In the Lübeck Orphanage* (fig. 2). The work at first seems to consist of three scenes from the Lübeck orphanage, representing the charitable work of this Christian institution in the sacral form of an altarpiece. The left wing shows the large hall of the orphanage, probably during the school day, with girls sitting on benches reading. On the right wing, the girls process through the corridor of the orphanage holding hymnbooks, while a pastor in the typical frilled ruff collar watches over them from the door. The central panel shows the kitchen at mealtime. While the wings do in fact depict rooms from the orphanage at Lübeck Cathedral, the kitchen is that of the almshouse at the former Saint Anne's Priory. Thus the work is not a specific portrait of the Lübeck orphanage; rather, Kuehl presents us with the overarching narrative of an orphanage as a virtuous social institution, offering everything from education to victuals to training in the Christian faith. In so doing, he combines rooms from two different institutions, though this fact remained hidden to viewers unfamiliar with the place.

Kuehl's painting from 1894 (cat. 8) shows a less orchestrated, more spontaneous-seeming glimpse of life in the orphanage. Through historic photographs and documents, we are well informed as to the appearance of the rooms and exterior of the Lübeck orphanage. A postcard with a combination of various interior views exemplifies the message such late nineteenth-century images of the orphanage were intended to convey: the captions "Ess-Saal" (dining hall) and "Beschäftigung" (activity) refer to the benefits provided, while the panel in the "Vorsteher Sitzungs-Saal" (directors' meeting room) with the family coats of arms of previous directors impressively illustrate the institution's long tradition.[16] The painting by Kuehl shows the room designated "activity." The extent to which the artist oriented himself to the photo in the perspective and arrangement of the figures is remarkable; in particular, the figure of the girl with her chin in her hand, pressing a dimple into her cheek with her thumb, seems to have been taken directly from the photographic image.

The addition of details such as the flowers, the view from the window, and the overall sense of light and color makes Kuehl's painted version of the motif far more atmospheric than the photograph. Moreover, it conveys not only a warm, sunny, airy mood, but also a genre-like narrative: the girls read or knit, while the boys play chess or work with a fretsaw. In this respect, the orphanage scene seems like a continuation of Liebermann's images of working processes, such as *Women Plucking Geese*. In Kuehl's composition, however, the figures enter into a relationship with each other—or rather, into a telling nonrelationship. And he uses the open doorway in the background to suggest a deeper narrative level: beyond the confines of the orderly activity of the schoolroom, a boy clambers up a tall cupboard, perhaps in search of better toys.

The scheme of an open door in the background exposing the view of an additional room—and an additional level of the narrative—was something

Kuehl could have learned from seventeenth-century Dutch genre painters. In comparison to Liebermann's pictures of the same theme, Gotthardt Kuehl strives to convey an overall image of the orphanage that is more than just a charming, picturesque scene. In this way, his pictorial narratives contribute to the positive, self-confident presentation of the bourgeois society of his time as a success story. In this respect, too, he stands in the tradition of seventeenth-century Dutch painters.

Elegant Material: Genre Painting with Modern Themes

In his later Impressionist work, Liebermann largely distanced himself from narrative genre scenes. When Emil Heilbut once again wrote about Liebermann in 1903, he remarked that the artist had turned to more elegant material for his genre painting: riding, tennis, and polo.[17] Liebermann's *Tennis Players by the Sea* (fig. 4) does in fact seem like a snapshot of casual bourgeois recreation. The net running diagonally through the picture and the informal placement of the players on either side of it make the scene appear as if glimpsed by chance. This quality becomes especially noticeable if we compare the work with another tennis picture, Ferdinand Brütt's *Tennis Match in Bad Homburg* from 1904 (fig. 5). Like Kuehl, Brütt had begun his career painting classical, bucolic, and anecdotal genre scenes. He had studied in Weimar from 1870 to 1876, worked in Düsseldorf from 1876 to 1898, and moved to Kronberg in the Taunus in 1898.[18] In nearby Bad Homburg, a tennis club had been founded in 1879, and it was there that Brütt found the motif for his modern bourgeois genre scene in 1904.

5
Ferdinand Brütt,
Tennis Match in Bad Homburg, 1904,
Städel Museum, Frankfurt am Main

Unlike Liebermann, Brütt does not position the net diagonally. The picture shows a little more than half of the tennis court, seen from a vantage point slightly to the left of the net. The court is framed by spectators seated close together as well as by a dense row of trees in the background. Brütt designs this open-air scene in classical, stage-like fashion, with a backdrop parallel to the picture plane and the ground extending all the way to the lower edge of the picture. But what story is this tennis scene meant to tell? To the left, one of the players is just winding up to hit the ball to the right. Our instinct is to follow its path, but the right half of the court is outside the composition. The symmetrical pictorial structure allows us to easily imagine it, due above all to our vantage point near the central axis of the court. The movement involved in the game, the "back and forth," is thus implied by the composition, though only a small section is actually shown. The further progress of the game lies outside the picture and has to be imagined by the viewer. This scheme reflects the classical approach of genre painting in which only a single moment of the narrative is depicted, leaving it up to the viewer to supply the "before" and "after."

In light of the social function of tennis, this genre scene can also be read as a piece of social commentary. In his study *Der Sport* (Sports) from 1908, Robert Hessen observed that "in a certain respect, tennis courts [were] more bountiful even than ballrooms" and described the gatherings there as "a rational extension of the marriage market."[19] The audience arranged around the tennis court in bright colors alludes to this aspect. The reinterpretation of classical genre scenes using modern themes and Impressionist brushwork played an important role in painting around 1900.

Another picture by Ferdinand Brütt also bespeaks the reception of the roots of such bourgeois, Impressionistic genre scenes. As mentioned earlier, Brütt had spent twelve years in Düsseldorf and was probably quite familiar with the genre painting of the Düsseldorf School. In 1900 he chose a highly modern motif for his painting *A Meeting of the Board of Directors* (fig. 6). His handling of this contemporaneous form of entrepreneurial leadership seems very traditional: in a dark interior dramatically lit by a ceiling lamp, nine men have gathered around a table to examine some business papers. A gentleman with a long beard, probably the chairman leading the discussion, has risen to speak, pointing to several of the documents in front of him. The other participants are grouped around the table in differing postures, showing varying degrees of interest: one bends forward, another reads the newspaper, while the young man next to the director looks thoughtfully at the documents, resting his head in his hand. Two of the others are engaged in a separate conversation, and the man in the left foreground even appears to have fallen asleep.

In his pictorial approach, Brütt echoes a painting from almost sixty years earlier, *The Reading Room* by Johann Peter Hasenclever (fig. 7). Here, on the eve of the revolution of 1848, Hasenclever portrayed a group of educated citizens reading the daily press. He depicted a variety of types and characters: calm, pensive, or concentrated readers as well as those who had dozed off over their papers. In Brütt's painting, the educated class of the early nineteenth century, whom Hasenclever had portrayed amid the atmospheric glow of a gas lamp, now yields to the propertied class, illuminated by modern, functional electric lighting. For Brütt, Impressionist brushwork and the staging of the motif in artificial light were the contemporary painterly means suitable for an image with an element of social criticism.

6
Ferdinand Brütt,
A Meeting of the Board of Directors, 1900,
Hamburger Kunsthalle

7
Johann Peter Hasenclever,
The Reading Room, 1843,
Alte Nationalgalerie, Berlin

Max Liebermann and the Linde Family in Lübeck

Around 1900 Liebermann's aforementioned painting *The Dutch Sewing School* (fig. 3) belonged to the private collection of Lübeck ophthalmologist Max Linde. In the magazine *Kunst und Künstler,* Emil Heilbut wrote about Linde's collection, which included works by Edgar Degas, Édouard Manet, and Pierre-Auguste Rodin as well as a portrait of the collector painted by Liebermann.[20] Linde's father, Hermann Linde Sr., was a photographer, and Max's younger brothers Hermann Jr. and Heinrich Eduard Walther were painters. The latter worked under the name Linde-Walther; his painting *Child in a Playroom* (cat. 82) captures a fleeting scene that is Impressionistic to the letter. The room in which the child stands is probably more of a salon or a dining room than a playroom; with her toys spread out before her, she is now distracted by the painter's presence. She turns toward him with a gaze that seems both curious and shy; at the same time, the interruption of her childlike play gives her a hesitant, almost sad demeanor. In the completed painting, her eyes meet ours, and we seem to have disturbed her game. How much Linde-Walther's pictures were conceived with the viewer in mind is illustrated by a final example.

After his initial training as a photographer in Vienna, Linde-Walther worked for two years as a colorist and retoucher in Cairo before studying painting in Munich from 1891 to 1894 and in Paris until 1897. Through his brother Max's connections to Liebermann, he moved to Berlin and became an official member of the Secession in 1901. In 1902 Linde-Walther painted *The Hartengrube in Lübeck* (fig. 8), an unspectacular yet picturesque view of a street in the historic town center of Lübeck. He augmented the cityscape of gabled houses and red roofs with staffage figures—a mother and her young daughter—and in so doing incorporated not only a narrative but also a reception-related aesthetic element into the painting.[21] The mother, her gaze lowered, approaches the right edge of the picture; the middle ground also shows passersby who seem unaware of either their surroundings or the painter. The little girl in the foreground, however, breaks through this otherwise anonymous street scene. With an expression of curiosity—perhaps a little fearful but at the same time brave—she looks out of the picture, directly to where the painter has posted himself with his easel. Two kindred gazes now meet: the little girl's curious, unbiased look and the artistic vision of the painter, who has recognized a picture-worthy motif in an ordinary stretch of street. In this way, Linde-Walther captures the impression of a modern city with an unsullied gaze like that of a child.

Yet when Linde-Walther exhibited the painting at the Berlin Secession in 1903, it had a very different appearance. The original version showed not a mother and daughter, but a gentleman with a riding crop and straw hat in the foreground, peering skeptically at the painter. Ultimately, Linde-Walther seems to have been dissatisfied with the figure of the man, whose expression betrays complete incomprehension of Impressionist plein-air painting. The artist altered the picture, erased the critic of his painting, and replaced him with an ally in the form of a child.

8
Heinrich Eduard Linde-Walther,
The Hartengrube in Lübeck, 1902,
Museum Behnhaus Drägerhaus, Lübeck

9
Edgar Degas,
Place de la Concorde, 1875,
Hermitage, Saint Petersburg

Conclusion

This final example suggests the extent to which Impressionism, or plein-air painting in general, still met with incomprehension outside the art world, even after 1900. The classically educated bourgeoisie still expected paintings to depict edifying, historical, or literary scenes. German artists of the modern generation, however, wanted to emulate their French colleagues. Linde-Walther's *Hartengrube,* for example, also echoes a French model: Degas's *Place de la Concorde* of 1875 (fig. 9). In fact, Linde-Walther was probably quoting the figure of the gentleman moving rightward out of the picture, umbrella tucked under his left arm—but with a decisive difference: no one in Degas's picture takes any notice of us. There, like a flaneur, the artist moves unseen through the streets of Paris, an unobserved observer of city life, not entering into dialogue with any of the figures in the painting. In his image of the *Hartengrube,* on the other hand, Linde-Walther becomes an interactive observer. The device of a figure gazing out from the group and drawing the viewer into the reception of the picture, employed in many of the Impressionist visual narratives discussed above, once again shows how important seventeenth-century Dutch painting was as a model. There, this compositional strategy had been used above all in group portraits such as the *Banquet of the Officers of the Saint Hadrian Civic Guard Company* by Frans Hals (fig. 10). Such painting "presupposes the beholding subject by allowing the figures to make direct contact with him through gaze, gesture, and movement."[22] In genre painting, the beholder is presupposed as the completer of the pictorial narrative; the gaze that draws us into the picture also invites us to continue the story. In this way, Holland was also significant as a model for this special type of visual narrative in German Impressionism, and along with France served as an important point of reference for painters such as Liebermann, Kuehl, and Linde-Walther.

Translated from German by Melissa M. Thorson

10
Frans Hals,
Banquet of the Officers of the Saint Hadrian Civic Guard Company, 1627,
Frans Hals Museum, Haarlem

Karoline Feulner

From Wild Garden to Stage

The Impressionism of Max Slevogt in Berlin and Neukastel

The idyllic manor of Neukastel above the small wine village of Leinsweiler in the Palatinate became Max Slevogt's adopted home and the place where he created many of his Impressionist landscapes. He had known the estate since his youth, since it belonged to the family of his wife, Antonie Finkler, due to his extensive connections to them through relatives.[1] Slevogt (fig. 3), who was born and raised in Bavaria, completed his studies at the academy in Munich and subsequently sought to establish himself as an artist there. It was Paul Cassirer, Max Liebermann, and Walter Leistikow who persuaded Slevogt to join the Berlin Secession, and the resulting move from Munich to Berlin was a turning point for him. From 1901 on, he commuted between Berlin and the Palatinate,[2] and the exposure to the rapidly changing art scene in Berlin had a profound influence on his work. Yet his oeuvre was also shaped by motifs from the Neukastel manor (also later known as Slevogthof), which he acquired in 1914. At his home in the Palatinate, Slevogt created a refuge from the hustle and bustle of Berlin where he could enjoy a secluded life. His garden and the view of the Rhine valley from his terrace became the subject of countless paintings. Such works, created under varying conditions of light and weather and at every season of the year, established his reputation as an Impressionist landscape painter. The interplay of influences from Berlin and Neukastel in the Impressionist painting of Max Slevogt is the subject of this essay.

Artists and Gardens

Like Slevogt, Max Liebermann, too, created a distinctive realm at his private home, the Liebermann Villa in Wannsee. Both the Slevogthof and the Liebermann Villa were designed in accord with their owners' wishes and thus reflect the artists' differing characters. Liebermann began laying out his garden after purchasing the property in 1909.[3] Elaborately designed and clearly structured, it is divided into a kitchen garden and a lawn facing the lake with a flower terrace, hedge gardens, and an avenue of birches. The kitchen garden is articulated by a central path with adjoining separate beds for flowers and vegetables. Everything is geometrically ordered, with direct lines of sight from the house to the lake. The garden on the lakeside is dominated by a large lawn with straight paths on either side, while the flowerbeds in front of the terrace are carefully bordered with boxwood. The lawn was well manicured, the trees regularly trimmed, and the hedge gardens meticulously pruned.[4] For Liebermann, nature was ordered and cultivated through and through in accord with his clear design; in this ensemble, the garden can be understood as a kind of architectural unit.

Slevogt's paintings, in contrast, show a view into the overgrown, seemingly enchanted idyll of his large estate of Neukastel.[5] Here there are no clear paths, axes, or structures; everything appears lush and wild, a true paradise of flora and fauna. The grape-laden vines and garden corner with a stone table, for example, served him as a motif more than once.[6] In the early 1920s, Slevogt added a wing toward the south, the library with a music room, which he adorned with elaborate frescoes. The music room is decorated with scenes from his favorite operas by Richard Wagner and Wolfgang Amadeus Mozart, while the library ceiling shows the principal heroes of his illustration projects: Macbeth, Achilles, Leatherstocking, and Scheherazade telling the sultan her tales for a thousand and one nights.[7] As his studio, Slevogt primarily used the adjoining terrace with its view of the Rhine valley, but he also worked in the garden or at the living room table.[8] From 1928 on, his extravagant refuge was enhanced by numerous sandstone figures of exuberant grape-bearing putti, designed by the master of the house and executed by a sculptor, though the stairway from the garden to the library was also lined by an African guard with a spear and an exotic woman lying beneath a palm tree with a sleeping leopard—figures seemingly taken from his illustrations to *The Arabian Nights.* This very personal design represented his pictorial worlds and at the same time embodied his own unique cosmos, composed of nature, music, and literature.

1
Max Slevogt,
The Garden in Neukastel with the Library, 1930–31,
Landesmuseum Mainz

2
Claude Monet,
The Garden at Vétheuil, 1881,
Hasso Plattner Collection,
Museum Barberini, Potsdam

Like his wild garden, Slevogt refused to be constrained by rules, contracts, or stipulations. He preferred to paint spontaneously, whenever a motif captured his interest. Karl Scheffler described this approach as "fitful, intuitive, and improvisational: he worked with incredible speed and concentration. A portrait, a still life, was often finished in just a few hours. As a draftsman, he was a night owl."[9] Slevogt preferred to choose his own subjects, such as for book projects, and when his publisher Bruno Cassirer asked him for new ideas for illustrations, he might deny the request, wishing only to produce paintings at that moment.[10] Bruno Cassirer reports that the artist was not always easy to work with, and that he was always full of new inspirations and surprises: "Texts that are suggested to him, he never actually illustrates."[11] On the other hand, if an idea seized him, he might draw it in just a few hours in the course of a single night—as occurred, for example, with the illustrations for the *Leatherstocking Tales* by James Fenimore Cooper, a book for young people that chanced to come into his hands again.[12] Such habits contrasted starkly with those of the highly disciplined Max Liebermann, who by his own testimony worked in his studio with the "regularity of a church clock."[13]

Painted Light

The private garden as a place of retreat, however, was an artistic motif derived above all from French Impressionism. Slevogt's painting of *The Garden in Neukastel with the Library* from 1930–31 (fig. 1), for example, recalls *The Garden at Vétheuil* by Claude Monet from 1881 (fig. 2). The painting by Monet was on view at the Kunstsalon Cassirer, the same gallery that represented Slevogt, and was acquired by Paul Cassirer;[14] thus it is highly likely that Slevogt knew it. But the artist's orientation to French Impressionism is also apparent in the similarity between his views of the Villa Godramstein, the country house of his wife's parents, and works such as Édouard Manet's 1882 painting of *The House at Rueil* (fig. p. 226), which Hugo von Tschudi had acquired for the Nationalgalerie in Berlin in 1906.[15] References of this kind should by no means be interpreted as quotations or appropriations, nor are there any books or photos in Slevogt's estate from which he might have copied directly. The same holds true for his small collection of art, which shows his interest in French modernism and included works by the artists most important to him: in addition to prints by Gustave Courbet, Honoré Daumier, and Eugène Delacroix, he also owned a painting by Manet.[16]

Slevogt's works inspired by French art are free adaptations in which he continued to develop impulses from abroad in his own style of painting. One of his contemporaries, art critic Julius Norden, wrote the following regarding his *Summer Morning* (fig. 4): "Looking at this plein-air painting, in which there were great difficulties to be overcome, one immediately thinks of Manet. But one also immediately recognizes how idiosyncratic it is, and how important this idiosyncrasy is, and that the Munich artist's palette is more luminous, more sparkling than that of the famous Parisian."[17]

Slevogt first encountered French art in 1889 during his semester abroad at the Académie Julian in Paris.[18] His exposure to Impressionism, however, was the result above all of the influence of Bruno and Paul Cassirer. In 1899 the two cousins boldly exhibited thirty-five works by Slevogt at their Kunstsalon together with the greats of French painting Edgar Degas, Édouard Manet, and Pierre Puvis de Chavannes.[19] Along with Manet's famous *The Luncheon on the Grass* (fig. p. 23), *The House at Rueil* by the same artist was also on view. And it was Paul Cassirer—one of the most innovative dealers open to modernism—who brought the French artists to Berlin and presented them to a wider public for the first time, assisted by his outstanding contacts in the Paris art and gallery scene. But Bruno and Paul Cassirer were also active as secretaries in the artists' association of the Berlin Secession and thus exerted a major influence on the choice of works exhibited there. They made the most of this influence and, as in the case of Max Slevogt, actively pursued the artists they deemed suitable. Paul Cassirer also suggested to Slevogt, who was only thirty-one at the time, that he view several private collections in Paris, including those of art dealer Paul Durand-Ruel and collectors George Viau and Alexandre Bernheim.[20] It was through these contacts that Slevogt, who at that time was still living in the artistically conservative city of Munich and struggling in vain for success, encountered French Impressionists such as Degas, Manet, and Monet.

When Slevogt returned to Paris in 1900 for the World's Fair, these recommendations from Cassirer were in his pocket. The occasion for his visit was the exhibition of his painting *Scheherazade* (1897, Neue Pinakothek, Munich) at the German pavilion and its receipt of a *Mention honorable*—an important international debut for the newcomer.[21] While there is no proof that he followed Cassirer's advice and pursued the contacts in Paris, it is certain that he later saw French Impressionist works in numerous exhibitions at the Kunstsalon Cassirer and that his painting underwent a significant change in the years that followed. The only evidence for any direct exposure to Impressionism in France is a postcard Slevogt wrote to art collector Carl Steinbart in 1910, in which he implies that during previous visits to Paris, he had looked at "new art": "Paris was mentally refreshing and was very good for me. This time,

3
Max Slevogt,
A Self-Portrait in the Garden at Godramstein, 1910,
Worcester Art Museum

4
Max Slevogt,
Summer Morning, 1901,
Landesmuseum Mainz

however, I did not look at any new art at all, and so cannot say what is 'going on' there . . . ."[22]

Like all the works he created and exhibited in Munich, the *Scheherazade* honored in Paris was still entirely indebted to the dark-toned studio painting of the Munich academy. A change in his style occurred shortly before his first documented contact with the Cassirers, who wanted to take him under contract:[23] in the garden at Neukastel, Slevogt created the first of his works that could be described as Impressionist-influenced in terms of both painterly approach and motif, executed *alla prima* in the open air. In 1898, for example, he painted *Flowering Trees in Neukastel* and *Bed of Roses and White Girl*, and a year later *Nini on the Wall—Plein-Air Study* (all three in private collections). The latter work was exhibited multiple times by the Cassirers; in a letter to Nini Slevogt, Bruno Cassirer requested it for an exhibition: "I think the picture is of such extraordinary beauty that we cannot do without it at all, if, as we intend, we want to show the current state of German painting next month."[24]

5
Édouard Manet,
Jean-Baptiste Faure in the Opera "Hamlet" by Ambroise Thomas, 1877,
Hamburger Kunsthalle

In *Flowering Trees,* Slevogt used confident, sketch-like brushstrokes to capture the white blossoms shimmering in the sunlight, while the leaves of the trees are merely suggested with numerous daubs of paint; the picture evokes a play of light and backlight, shadow and brightness, against a landscape vista that dissolves into color. Slevogt had now moved on from the works he had created only a few years earlier such as *Wrestling School* (1893, Landesmuseum Mainz) or *Danaë* (1895, Städtische Galerie im Lenbachhaus und Kunstbau, Munich), which depicted figural compositions that seem bulky. In comparison to these realistic paintings, rendered in a rougher, darker tonality with coarse brushstrokes that were often described as "brutal" by contemporary critics, the artist seems to have reinvented himself.[25] Moreover, he did not paint them in a studio in Munich, but in the undisturbed seclusion of his own private garden.

Exposure to works of French Impressionism, which Slevogt now also saw in Berlin, reinforced this direction. He experimented with this radically new approach in works such as the ones created at the Frankfurt Zoo in 1901 and subsequently made paintings such as *Summer Morning* (fig. 4), an ode to a glorious summer day and a celebration of leisure showing his wife, Nini, with a large parasol, lying at a bold diagonal in the midst of the Palatinate Forest with its typical heather and pines. Here, too, the motif and its interpretation recall French models, while the large scale of the work helped the "new" artist achieve his breakthrough at the Berlin Secession. Compared to previous thematic or mythological compositions such as the *Wrestling School,* which Slevogt had presented in exhibitions and which were indebted to Realism and history painting, *Summer Morning* exemplifies the complete change of style that would enable him to attain success. It would be an oversimplification, however, to limit his influences to those from France: Arnold Böcklin, Francisco de Goya, Frans Hals, Wilhelm Leibl, and Rembrandt also served as important artistic points of reference for him.

Dance and Opera

As much as Slevogt relished the quiet seclusion and inexhaustible inspiration for his landscapes he found in the Palatinate, he also needed a counterpole. The bustling metropolis of Berlin afforded him other themes and ideas, and above all offered concerts, operas, theater and dance performances, vaudeville, and the cinema, which he especially loved. Moreover, as one of the leading artists of the Berlin Secession, he was connected with a network of dealers and artists. His works were promoted, for example, in the magazine *Kunst und Künstler* published by Bruno Cassirer, and Slevogt regularly gathered with other artists at the Romanisches Café. The Berlin art scene also gave Slevogt access to an intellectual milieu: he was acquainted with leading scientists such as Albert Einstein and Fritz Haber and painted portraits of major politicians and businessmen of his day.[26]

Slevogt had musical talent and at first wanted to become an opera singer. But he was also a gifted dancer who frequented masquerade and artists' balls even during his time in Munich.[27] Female dancers are a central motif in his oeuvre. The two paintings *Dancer in Gold* and *Dancer in Silver* (cats. 109, 110) were created while he was still in Munich and are characterized by a darker palette. Both compositions also bear witness to the influence of Jugendstil, in which dance was a leitmotif and a symbol of joie de vivre, as well as Symbolism, represented in Munich by Franz von Stuck. These early works not only exemplify Slevogt's turn away from the conservative visual world of the Munich academy and his exploration of the Jugendstil themes typical of the time but also show his development of a style of painting based increasingly on color. The woman in *Dancer in Silver* wears a veil-thin dress rendered in almost transparent hues, ranging from violet to green. The ecstatic figure is shrouded in confident, impasto brushstrokes, as if enveloped by the color harmony. In *Dancer in Gold,* the thickly applied strokes of gold create individual reflections of light that seem to cascade down the figure. The motif of dance would remain a constant for Slevogt, who was interested above all in exotic performances and created striking role portraits of famous female dancers such as Japanese kabuki actor Sada Yacco, Russian ballerina Anna Pavlova, and flamenco dancer Marietta Rigardo.

6
Max Slevogt,
The Champagne Aria from "Don Giovanni," 1902,
Niedersächsisches Landesmuseum Hannover

Slevogt's best-known role portrait is probably that of Portuguese baritone Francisco d'Andrade as Don Giovanni (cats. 114–16). In 1901 the artist had seen him perform in the Mozart opera at the Theater des Westens in Berlin and subsequently created a number of paintings based on his impressions.[28] Slevogt had already been enthralled by the singer's ability at a performance in Munich in 1894, and over the years he developed a friendship with the baritone, who for him was the consummate embodiment of Don Giovanni. In the portrait *The Champagne Aria* (cat. 115), the singer seems to merge with his role: the beaming hero, raising his glove in his right hand, has triumphantly sung the last note of the aria and receives the well-deserved adulation of the audience. After rejecting his original idea for a monumental stage painting (fig. 6), Slevogt developed the composition in numerous small sketches, some of which have been preserved in the artist's estate. Drawn in his typical fashion on the backs of envelopes, telegrams, or other slips of paper, they enable us to trace the development of the work step by step.

The full-figure composition of an actor immersed in his role, standing at center stage, once again recalls a famous painting by Manet: *Jean-Baptiste Faure in the Opera "Hamlet" by Ambroise Thomas* (fig. 5).[29] Although we can only speculate as to whether Slevogt knew this particular work, whether in the original or as a reproduction, it is certain that Manet was the French artist who had the strongest influence on Slevogt. As early as 1902, when Slevogt's *The Champagne Aria* drew admiration at the exhibition of the Berlin Secession, critic Hans Rosenhagen made a general observation as to the importance of Manet's example: "Here, one can probably no longer speak of the direct influence of Manet. Slevogt's talent is completely equal to the task at hand; yet contact with Manet has ennobled his means of expression, which serves to his advantage and allows the painter to appear more remarkable than ever as an artistic personality. This d'Andrade may rightly be considered the 'highlight' of the exhibition."[30] Here, Slevogt combines the ideas of French Impressionism, new to him at the time, with his passion for music and his painterly virtuosity. Slevogt's role portrait *The Champagne Aria* established a new type to which he would return again and again in multiple variations. Along with *Summer Morning*, the work stands for Slevogt's initiation into the world of the Berlin Secession and marks his breakthrough after many setbacks in Munich: like the triumphantly beaming d'Andrade, he had now arrived on the big stage.

7
Édouard Manet,
Bundle of Asparagus, 1880,
Wallraf-Richartz-Museum & Fondation Corboud, Cologne

8
Édouard Manet,
The Melon, ca. 1880,
National Gallery of Art, Washington

"The King of Illustration"

To reduce Max Slevogt to painting alone would not do him justice: he was an extremely prolific illustrator who produced numerous narrative images for his publisher Bruno Cassirer, based on sources such as *The Arabian Nights* or the fairy tales of the Brothers Grimm. Yet his creativity and inventiveness were also manifested in illustrations for adventure novels such as the *Leatherstocking Tales,* classics such as Johann Wolfgang von Goethe's *Faust II* (with 510 lithographs created for the latter alone), and the portfolio *The Magic Flute: Marginal Drawings on Mozart's Manuscript.* Slevogt's innovative book illustrations also reflect many aspects of Impressionism, such as the rapid, lively style in which they are drawn, capturing the characters in "high-action," snapshot-like scenes. In the chalk lithographs in particular, he perfects a fine tonality that gives rise to tremendous atmospheric effect or adds a painterly, impressionistic landscape to the background. As one of the best-known printmakers and illustrators of his day, he earned the title "king of illustration."[31] He also created numerous costume studies and stage designs for productions such as Mozart's *Don Giovanni* and painted frescoes including *Golgotha,* a monumental Passion scene executed in the Friedenskirche in Ludwigshafen in 1932.

Slevogt's personality cannot be grasped apart from his sense of humor, which came to expression in the marginal drawings of his letters or the menu cards he created for special occasions. His design for the title page of the menu for Paul Cassirer's fiftieth birthday shows a waiter holding a tray with a single stalk of asparagus and comparing it to the painting *Bundle of Asparagus* by Édouard Manet (fig. 7) on an easel.[32] The latter was in the art collection of Max Liebermann, as was Manet's *The Melon* from around 1880 (fig. 8), which appears on the floor to the right in the drawing.[33] In the background, the guests boisterously dance around a single, erect stalk of asparagus, while another is added to the left in a kind of parody of the dance around the Golden Calf.[34] With the *Bundle of Asparagus,* Slevogt is quoting not just any painting, but one that programmatically represented both his own and Liebermann's conception of art. In this view, any object—no matter how banal, like a simple bunch of asparagus—could serve as a motif for a masterpiece, ranking equally alongside much weightier themes. For Liebermann, it was "imagination" that "alone turns craft into art," understood as the "enlivening spirit of the artist, hidden behind every stroke of his work."[35] As a colorist, Slevogt embraced this conception of art, in which composition, color, and the application of paint were more important than the content or symbolic significance of the objects. He created still lifes that consisted of a single pineapple, a cut-open watermelon, a crude bowl of sausages, or simply oranges in crystal bowls (fig. 9; see also cats. 92, 93, 97–99).[36] His painted fruits and flowers are modeled by means of color and celebrate the fleeting moment; they show the beauty of the everyday and the small. It is no longer the object itself that is of primary interest but the fundamental experience of seeing—a principle that remains the leitmotif of his Impressionist works. Slevogt painted the things "that make the world so beautiful." For as he himself stated, "Anyone who doesn't already see the color in life won't be able to see a picture that's painted impressionistically."[37]

Translated from German by Melissa M. Thorson

9
Max Slevogt,
Still Life with Oranges, 1920,
private collection

10
Max Slevogt,
Still Life with Lemons, 1921,
Alte Nationalgalerie, Berlin

Lucy Wasensteiner

Max Liebermann

Painter and Collector of Impressionism

In May 1927 seventy-nine-year-old Max Liebermann published an obituary for recently deceased Claude Monet in the magazine *Kunst und Künstler.* The text makes evident how Liebermann defined Impressionism at that point in his career and which artists he associated with the movement. He wrote:

> *The passing of Claude Monet forever closes the circle that joined him to his great compatriots Manet, Degas, Renoir, Cézanne, Pissarro, and Sisley under the name "The Impressionists": differing enormously from each other in talent and temperament, yet resembling each other in one thing, that they, as born painters, saw their ideal in the imitation of nature. They wanted to paint not religious or historical pictures, not landscapes or still lifes, but what they saw . . . ; in short, they were naive, or wanted to be as naive as possible.*[1]

In the century since the publication of Liebermann's essay, countless other definitions of Impressionism have been proposed. Yet the artists associated with this term, ambiguous as it is, have remained largely the same, and include—along with Monet—Édouard Manet, Edgar Degas, Pierre-Auguste Renoir, Paul Cézanne, Camille Pissarro, and Alfred Sisley. With the exception of Manet, all were represented in the first exhibition of the Société Anonyme des Artistes Peintres, Sculpteurs, Graveurs, etc. (Anonymous Society of Painters, Sculptors, Engravers, etc.) in Paris in 1874, which became known as the first Impressionist exhibition.[2] Although he did not participate in the aforementioned show, Manet had already established himself as a central protagonist in the movement in the late 1860s through his participation in the Salon des Refusés.

The imitation of nature without recourse to religious or historical motifs is clearly recognizable in the late works of Max Liebermann, whether in his images of beach life in Holland, his Hamburg scenes of leisure activities, or the pictures of his garden in Wannsee (cats. 117–32). In the years after 1900, other parallels emerged between Liebermann's painting and the interests of the French artists he associated with Impressionism. Like the latter, Liebermann, too, preferred to paint *en plein air,* without making preparatory studies on paper. In order to capture the effect of the light, he used loose brushstrokes and bright hues, often with an impasto application of paint. And in his choice of motifs, he was increasingly inspired by the leisure activities of the bourgeoisie, whether convivial gatherings in beer gardens and pubs or the enjoyment of his own garden.

Liebermann had already acquired his first works by Manet and Degas in the 1890s. After 1900, his holdings grew through numerous purchases, and by the time of his death in 1935 he owned one of the most important private collections of French Impressionism in the world. But what specific Impressionist works did Max Liebermann acquire, and what connections can be discerned between his purchases and the development of his late work? Did the collection serve as direct inspiration for his own art, or did it fulfill other functions for the artist? The following essay elucidates the genesis and significance of Liebermann's Impressionist collection against the backdrop of the political turmoil of the late Kaiserreich, the Weimar Republic, and the rise of the Nazi Party. In so doing, it also illuminates the subsequent fate of the paintings amassed by Liebermann. Like many works of French Impressionism acquired by progressive Jewish collectors in Germany, some of the paintings from Liebermann's possession would also find their way into collections abroad after 1933.

1
Édouard Manet,
Madame Manet at Bellevue, 1880,
Metropolitan Museum of Art, New York

The Beginnings of the Collection

Max Liebermann grew up in a social and intellectual milieu in which appreciating and collecting art were the norm.[3] In the early nineteenth century, the Jewish Liebermann family had settled in Berlin, where the artist's ancestors founded successful textile businesses. In the mid-nineteenth century, his uncle Adolf Liebermann von Wahlendorf owned an extensive collection with works by contemporary German and French artists such as Adolph von Menzel, Camille Corot, Charles-François Daubigny, and Eugène Delacroix.[4] In 1857 Max Liebermann's father acquired the Stüler-Palais at Pariser Platz, one of the most prestigious addresses in the city. A further sign of the family's prosperity and cultural standing was the fact that the young Max did not have to enter the family business but was instead free to pursue an education as an artist. After completing his studies in painting at the Großherzoglich-Sächsische Kunstschule (Grand-Ducal Saxon Art School) in Weimar, Liebermann moved to Paris in 1873, where he lived for five years. Although he was present in the French capital when the first Impressionist exhibition was mounted in 1874, there is no indication that Liebermann visited the show; at the time, he was more interested in works from the Dutch tradition as well as the plein-air painting of the Barbizon School.[5]

Liebermann probably began building his collection during the 1870s. It is known, for example, that he acquired the watercolor *Liebermann's Paris Studio* (location unknown) by his friend Thomas Herbst in 1877, the year of its completion.[6] However, there is no evidence that these early purchases also included examples of French Impressionism. The first phase of significant growth for Liebermann's collection took place in the 1890s—precisely the time when he was at the forefront of making Impressionist painting known in Germany. About a year after his return to Berlin in 1884 (having spent the years since 1878 in Munich and the Netherlands), Liebermann became aware of the French Impressionist collection of Carl and Felicie Bernstein,[7] the earliest of its kind in the German capital.[8] Liebermann's increasing professional success soon made it possible for him to acquire Impressionist works himself. In 1892 he painted a portrait of collector Carl Bernstein, who in return gave him Manet's

Peonies (fig. 2).[9] The same year, he acquired Degas's pastel *The Respite* (ca. 1883, private collection) from Paris art dealer Paul Durand-Ruel.[10] Over the course of the 1890s, acquisitions of other works by Manet followed, including *The Melon* (fig. p. 56), *Madame Manet at Bellevue* (fig. 1), and *Rochefort's Escape* (1881, Kunsthaus Zurich).[11] In 1898, the year of the founding of the Berlin Secession, Liebermann also purchased Monet's work *Manet Painting in Monet's Garden in Argenteuil* (1874, location unknown) directly from Manet's widow.[12] The importance of French Impressionism in setting the course for the Berlin Secession early on is reflected in a succinct statement by Liebermann, written in retrospect in 1909: "The founding of the Secession was a sign of burgeoning life, a rebirth. . . . An aging art was replaced by one that was young and fresh: the art of Impressionism."[13]

New Purchases after 1900

In many respects, the first decade of the twentieth century represents the high point of Liebermann's career. His role in the Secession made him one of the best-known and most-influential figures in German cultural politics. Moreover, he was also extremely successful from a financial perspective, due in large measure to his popularity as a painter of society portraits. Liebermann's acquisition of Impressionist art continued at a rapid pace during this period. Around the turn of the century, he acquired Monet's *Windmills near Zaandam* (1871, Van Gogh Museum, Amsterdam).[14] Moreover, since the 1890s the Monet painting *Summer, Poppy Field* (fig. 8) had been present in his home, on loan from the Bernsteins; after the death of Felicie Bernstein in 1908, it was bequeathed to Liebermann by her estate.[15] Both of the aforementioned Monets find a visual echo in Liebermann's own work from between 1900 and 1910, especially in his loosely painted Dutch landscapes with their overcast skies or his brightly colored, summery beach scenes. Yet Liebermann was also interested in the interplay of landscape and figure in Monet's work. In a 1906 letter to Alfred Lichtwark, director of the Kunsthalle in Hamburg, Liebermann derided the idea of pure landscape painting as "madness," writing that "only figure painters can paint landscapes (proof: Cl. Monet . . .)."[16] About two decades later, in a text on Monet published in 1927, he emphasized this aspect once again—this time with reference to Goethe: "Goethe says: we know of no world except in relation to human beings, we want no art except as an impression of this relation."[17] Thus it is telling that in Liebermann's late Dutch landscapes, a human figure or a trace of human participation always constitutes the focus of the scene.

The interest in the connection between figure and landscape may also explain Liebermann's important purchases of works by Edgar Degas in the years after 1900. The pastel *Dancers with Fans* (ca. 1898, location unknown) was acquired in 1903 through his dealer Paul Cassirer, as was the monumental oil painting *Frieze of Dancers* (ca. 1895, Cleveland Museum of Art) a year later.[18] In the course of the decade, further acquisitions of ballet scenes followed, including *Dancers with a Chair* (ca. 1895, private collection), which Liebermann purchased in 1909.[19] At first glance, these works by Degas seem an unusual choice, since Liebermann's own oeuvre scarcely depicts the world of dance.[20] What he found so fascinating, though, was the specific focus on the representa-

2
Édouard Manet,
Peonies, 1882,
Murauchi Art Museum, Tokyo

3
Pierre-Auguste Renoir,
Flowers in a Greenhouse, 1864,
Hamburger Kunsthalle

tion of figures in space. Informative in this regard is a 1902 letter from Liebermann to Wilhelm von Bode, director of the Gemäldegalerie in Berlin, in which he says of Rembrandt: "[Rembrandt] composes not in space, but with space . . . just like Velasquez [*sic*] or Degas or—me."[21]

While there is little direct similarity between the works by Degas and Liebermann's oeuvre, it is entirely possible that Degas's studies of dancers provided Liebermann with inspiration for his own figural images. The importance of Renoir's floral still life *Flowers in a Greenhouse* (fig. 3), which Liebermann purchased in 1905, could be evaluated in a similar way.[22] Although floral still lifes occur only very seldom in Liebermann's oeuvre, it is quite possible that he drew inspiration for his own work from this purchase—especially with respect to the depiction of flora and fauna, which were important motifs in his paintings after 1900.

4
Édouard Manet,
Women at the Races, 1866,
Cincinnati Art Museum

Could it have been Liebermann's distinct interest in the representation of figures that prompted him to acquire Paul Cézanne's *The Fishermen (Fantastic Scene)* (fig. 6) in 1909?[23] Or should the purchase rather be understood as a show of solidarity with his friend, Hugo von Tschudi, who had recently been dismissed from his position as director of the Nationalgalerie in Berlin on account of his support for modern French painting? Tschudi had acquired the picture for the museum in 1908, but after his dismissal that same year it was sold again and was ultimately purchased by Liebermann through Cassirer in January 1909. Liebermann himself seems to have been uncertain as to whether the painting should be considered an example of French Impressionism, although the Tschudi provenance was unequivocal in that regard. Shortly after acquiring the picture, he wrote to Gustav Pauli, then director of the Kunsthalle in Bremen:

> *[I] bought the Cézanne with the white sail—the picture was with Tschudi for a year until his leave. You see: I am trying to improve my taste. . . . The picture is perhaps too much decoration and somewhat too little nature, almost Venetian, but it is—charming and—demolishes everything else. Perhaps those who consider Cézanne the greatest genius of the Impressionists (to which he did not belong at all) are right.*[24]

Liebermann's most extensive acquisitions after 1900 were from the oeuvre of Édouard Manet. After the turn of the century, at least ten Manets entered his collection, including *George Moore in the Artist's Garden* (fig. 5) and *Women at the Races* (fig. 4), both acquired in 1904, and the *Bundle of Asparagus* (fig. p. 56), acquired in 1907.[25] Not only was Manet one of the artists most represented in Liebermann's collection, he was also frequently discussed and praised in his letters and texts.[26] Among the latter are two essays by Liebermann printed in the aforementioned magazine *Kunst und Künstler*: a treatise on two Manet woodcuts, published in 1905, and a discussion of Manet's painting *The Execution of Emperor Maximilian* (1868–69, Kunsthalle Mannheim), published in 1910.[27] These articles clearly identify the special characteristics Liebermann appreciated in the work of Manet: the simplified quality of his forms and compositions,[28] the maintaining of a sketch-like freshness in the finished painting,[29] and the skillful handling of material and color. Liebermann admired Manet's "richness of color" and "fullness of tone" and rendered the verdict: "Only Rembrandt knew how to do so much with so little!"[30] These same features characterize Liebermann's most compelling works from this period, such as his depictions of the beach in Holland or the streets of the Jewish quarter in Amsterdam.

Collecting as a Statement Against Antisemitism

The question arises as to whether Liebermann's purchases of works by Manet were also politically motivated, an act of resistance against the growing antisemitism in Europe. One painting by Manet did in fact find its way into Liebermann's collection as the result of antisemitic attitudes. In the mid-1890s, when the trial against the Jewish artillery officer Alfred Dreyfus began in Paris, Liebermann made a bet with his friend Charles Ephrussi, a Paris banker and collector of Manet. Liebermann wagered that the case would be decided in Dreyfus's favor; Ephrussi was not convinced and was even willing to stake his Manet painting *Fishing Boat with Tailwind* (1864, private collection) on the opposite outcome.[31] The optimist Liebermann finally received the painting in 1902.

Letters from the artist reveal how Manet's works were used by the antisemitic press to prove Liebermann's "foreignness" as a Jew. On April 9, 1903, Liebermann wrote to his friend, critic Julias Elias:

> *Apropos Manet, today some antisemitic newspaper wrote that his—and of course my—way of viewing nature was un-German. The German supposedly contemplates nature lovingly as a pious Christian; while I, as a Semite, think M's superficial manner is beautiful.*[32]

5
Édouard Manet,
George Moore in the Artist's Garden, ca. 1879, National Gallery of Art, Washington

Here the attempt was apparently made to associate Manet's modernity with an alleged Jewish threat to European society. Such openly antisemitic voices may have confirmed Liebermann in his appreciation for Manet and made him even more determined to buy more of the French artist's works. The question also arises as to whether voices such as these prompted Liebermann to acquire the only work by Camille Pissarro known to have been in his collection. In 1903 Liebermann bought the oil painting *Houseboat on the Oise, Pontoise* (ca. 1866, Kunstmuseum St. Gallen).[33] Certainly it, too, reflected his painterly interests, such as human intervention in the landscape, the loosely applied paint, and the overcast sky. Yet the provenance of the Pissarro painting seems relevant as well: around the turn of the century, it was in the private collection of Émile Zola, whose inflammatory text *J'accuse . . . !* (1898) played a key role in the Dreyfus affair. After Zola's death, his collection was auctioned at the Hôtel Drouot in Paris in March 1903. There, Paul Cassirer acquired the painting *Houseboat on the Oise, Pontoise,* which entered the collection of Max Liebermann the same year. Pissarro's own Jewish heritage supports the thesis of a political motivation behind this acquisition.

Late Work in Wannsee

In the late 1910s, Liebermann's leadership in the modern art scene in Berlin increasingly came under fire. Initial serious differences of opinion within the Secession ultimately led to him stepping down from his position as president

in 1911.[34] These events coincided with the completion of the artist's summer house on the banks of the Wannsee in Berlin. Since the death of his parents, Liebermann and his family had lived in the town house at Pariser Platz. In 1909 Max and Martha acquired two parcels in the villa colony of Alsen on the shore of the Wannsee and consolidated them into a single property.[35] The house and garden, carefully planned by Liebermann in collaboration with architect Paul Otto Baumgarten and landscape architect Albert Brodersen, were completed in 1910. The outbreak of World War I amplified the importance of the estate for Liebermann's artistic and family life. When the war made it impossible for him to continue his annual trips to the Netherlands, Wannsee became the primary summer motif for the painter, who at that time was already sixty-seven years old.

In many respects, Liebermann's home and garden in Wannsee were a focusing lens for his progressive attitudes. In contrast to his residence at Pariser Platz, the rooms were bright and airy.[36] The spacious garden complex with its geometric design and planting scheme in color blocks reflected the newest ideas of the *Reformgartenbewegung* (garden reform movement), among whose adherents was Alfred Lichtwark, who assisted the painter in the design of his new garden.[37] The estate in Wannsee was also adorned with Liebermann's collection of modern art, including Manet's large-scale oil painting *Portrait of Mr. Arnaud on Horseback* (ca. 1875, Galleria d'Arte Moderna di Milano), which he acquired in 1913.[38] Some have suggested that because it was displayed in his private living spaces, Liebermann's collection remained largely hidden from the public;[39] this view, however, can be refuted by evidence. In the years following his departure from the Secession in 1911, Liebermann remained a prominent personality, due in part to his appointment as president of the Academy of the Arts in 1920. Accordingly, his residences were photographed multiple times for various publications.[40] Some of these images presented Liebermann's art collection, and not just in Wannsee: other photographs showed the French Impressionist works in the spaces at Pariser Platz. Furthermore, Liebermann enjoyed talking about his collection and allowed reproductions of the works to be published with clear indication of his ownership.[41] In the years after 1914, his collection of modern art became a trademark for the artist.

Can we thus interpret Liebermann's last major series, the garden paintings from Wannsee, as a final articulation of his commitment to Impressionism? As images of a garden—a human intervention in nature, often with visible figures of family members or gardeners (cats. 117–32)—they recall the qualities Liebermann admired in the landscapes of Monet. The depiction of figures in green space may also echo works by Degas and Renoir in Liebermann's collection. Moreover, the paintings from the Wannsee series show the same skillful combination of meticulous composition with the preservation of a sketch-like quality that Liebermann appreciated in the works of Manet. Yet at the same time, decisive differences can be also discerned between Liebermann's Wannsee pictures and the works of the French Impressionists. For example, it has been argued that in contrast to an artist such as Manet, Liebermann allows his figures to merge much more closely with their environment.[42] There are also garden paintings from the mid-1920s in which Liebermann's sketch-like approach and "richness of color" clearly go beyond his beloved French models.

6
Paul Cézanne,
The Fishermen (Fantastic Scene), ca. 1875,
Metropolitan Museum of Art, New York

7
Paul Cézanne,
Meadow and Farm of Jas de Bouffan, ca. 1885–87,
National Gallery of Canada, Ottawa

In this sense, his works are more comparable to those of younger contemporaries such as Erich Heckel or Karl Schmidt-Rottluff.

Liebermann's friends likewise observed similarities between the garden pictures of the 1920s and works that were stylistically closer to Post-Impressionism. The artist's purchases of French painting began to stagnate already in 1914, although it is unclear whether this decline was politically motivated due to the outbreak of war or reflected diminishing personal interest or the rising cost of such works.[43] However, there were still occasional late acquisitions, such as the oil painting *Meadow and Farm of Jas de Bouffan* by Cézanne (fig. 7), purchased in 1916. The similarities between this unequivocally Post-Impressionist picture and Liebermann's late work—especially the early summer Wannsee paintings from 1924 and 1925—were noted already by Erich Hancke, the artist's biographer, in the late 1940s.[44]

The Fate of the Collection

Max Liebermann's private collection of French Impressionism was an important source of inspiration for his late oeuvre. The qualities he appreciated and admired in the work of his French colleagues increasingly manifested themselves in his own painting, from the integration of figure and landscape to composition, color, and form. Yet the collection was more than just a source of stylistic inspiration. It also served a variety of other purposes: as a reminder of old friends, as an articulation of the artist's modernity, as a means of constructing his own personal brand, as bourgeois self-representation, and perhaps also as a statement against antisemitism.

Certainly it was Liebermann's awareness of the wide-ranging functions of his art collection that moved him to take measures to secure its future shortly after the rise of the Nazi Party. Though culturally assimilated in many respects, the Liebermann family—Max; his wife, Martha; and their daughter, Käthe—never tried to deny their Jewish identity.[45] Accordingly, their downfall occurred rapidly beginning in 1933. In April of that year, Liebermann's son-in-law, Kurt Riezler, was dismissed from his professorship in Frankfurt am Main; a month later, Liebermann himself was forced to resign from his post as honorary president of the Berlin Academy of the Arts. The turmoil of these years soon became too much for the aging artist: in the winter of 1934, Max Liebermann fell ill, and on February 8, 1935, he died at the age of eighty-seven. In 1938 his daughter, Käthe, was able to emigrate to New York with her husband, Kurt, and their daughter, Maria, who was twenty-one at the time. Only Martha Liebermann remained in Berlin. Initially she hesitated to leave her home city, but by the time she realized the gravity of the situation, the Nazi regime had blocked her emigration. Confronted with deportation, she committed suicide in March 1943 at the age of eighty-five.

In these desperate years before Martha's suicide, a number of works from the family collection were lost, sold by Martha Liebermann under the pressure of persecution, or stolen from the family. Today, over 180 objects from the collection of Max and Martha Liebermann are registered as lost, including works by Manet, Degas, and Monet.[46] Part of the collection, however, was able to "escape," as it were, from the Nazi regime. In May 1933, Max Liebermann sent fourteen works to be stored at the Kunsthaus Zurich.[47] Thirteen of them were from his collection of French Impressionism: six Manets, his two Cézannes, three of his dance scenes by Degas, Renoir's *Flowers in a Greenhouse*, and Monet's *Windmills near Zaandam*.[48] Five years later, Liebermann's daughter and her family were able to take other French works with them into American exile, including five pieces by Manet as well as Monet's *Summer, Poppy Field* (fig. 8).[49]

Due to the measures undertaken to preserve the works abroad, a considerable portion of the Liebermann collection remained intact during the years of persecution and war. The works held in Zurich were brought to the United States by Käthe Liebermann. There, in the years after 1945, they were able to contribute to the next chapter in the history of the international reception of French Impressionism.

Translated from German by Melissa M. Thorson

8
Claude Monet,
Summer, Poppy Field, 1875,
private collection

Valentina Plotnikova

Impressionism in Germany

First Steps

In the 1870s, academic studio painting set the tone for modern art in the German Empire. Initially, there was little appreciation of French Impressionism; artists instead found their role models in the Barbizon School. Further impetus was provided by the naturalistic approach of the Dutch Hague School. The social realities of life were depicted in a realistic, narrative form. Only from the 1890s onward did Impressionist plein-air painting gain acceptance and evolve in various centers, including Berlin, Weimar, Munich, and Dresden.

In the German Empire of the 1870s, both the state and the academy called for dark-toned paintings made in the studio. The developments of French Impressionism—studying lighting relationships and sketch-like brushwork—had only minimal influence on local art at first. Max Liebermann and his contemporaries, who sought new inspiration in Paris, primarily studied French Realism. They were enthusiastic about the work by artists of the Barbizon School such as Gustave Courbet, Camille Corot, and Jean-François Millet, who painted outdoors in order to faithfully reproduce the rural environment (fig. 1). Liebermann, too, explored motifs of the farming life in the artist village of Barbizon (fig. 2).

In addition to Barbizon, Holland became a place of inspiration. As early as 1871, Liebermann was painting everyday scenes of remote fishing and farming villages. He explained this fascination of more than forty years as follows: "Holland . . . seems boring at first glance: we have to discover its secret beauties first. Its beauty lies in its intimacy."[1] German artists considered the painters of the Hague School, such as Jozef Israëls, role models for a "genuine" art (fig. 3)—in contrast with the idealizing history painting of the academy. At the same time, there were Naturalist tendencies in contemporary literature—for example, in the dramas of Gerhart Hauptmann. The new impulses from the Barbizon and Hague Schools led to the emergence of Naturalist plein-air painting—a precursor of German Impressionism. Until the beginning of the twentieth century, it was called the "modern form of Naturalism."[2]

1
Jean-François Millet,
The Gleaners, 1857,
Musée d'Orsay, Paris

2
Max Liebermann,
Potato Harvest, 1875,
Kunstpalast Düsseldorf

Although Liebermann painted *Free Period in the Amsterdam Orphanage* (cat. 7) in his studio, he used studies that he had prepared on site. This painting is characterized by Naturalism: even the threads of the girls sewing can be seen. The patches of light distributed across the canvas are not found in the studies; Liebermann added this play of light when executing the painting. He was not focused on the effects of Impressionist painting of light but rather on the composition of the figures.

The motifs from Holland, such as *Saint Stephen's Poorhouse in Leiden* (cat. 16) and *Hospital Garden in Edam* (cat. 17), form a thematically coherent group of works. Liebermann was impressed by the country's progressive social welfare as well as its social life, architecture, and nature.[3] Like many painters in Germany, he focused on the social dimension of art and preserved a narrative structure.[4] In the painting *Saint Stephen's Poorhouse in Leiden,* which shows an old people's home for needy citizens, however, the surroundings are foregrounded. The façade towers over the silent figures; the garden becomes the main stage. This painting is one of the earliest examples of the motif of a garden that Liebermann later made one of his central subjects.[5]

Fritz von Uhde, too, explored plein-air painting in Holland: in 1882, he visited the fishing village of Zandvoort, presumably influenced by Liebermann.[6] There, Uhde began the studies for *The Hurdy-Gurdy Man Is Coming* (cat. 5). The scene recalls a film sequence: the narrative impulses emanate from the hurdy-gurdy man who is walking through the garden gate. The children interrupt their play and race up to him.

Liebermann's *Free Period in the Amsterdam Orphanage* triggered such enthusiasm in Germany that a whole "sewing girl genre" evolved.[7] These works combine impulses from seventeenth-century Dutch genre painting with Naturalist plein-air painting, such as Uhde's *Dutch Sewing Room* (cat. 4). Gotthardt Kuehl also found motifs in orphanages and craft workshops. In *Orphans in Lübeck* (cat. 9), the artist remains faithful to a genre-like narrative. Three girls are absorbed by their handiwork, while a fourth is pausing for a moment. The empty chair on the right suggests that the person in charge is absent. Once again, the artist's primary interest is not the play of light but the narrative of the pictorial motif.

3
Jozef Israëls,
Woman Knitting, 1876,
private collection

The 1890s marked a turning point in the evolution toward Impressionism. Liebermann began to brighten his palette; his brushwork became looser. He turned from everyday scenes from people's lives and toward depicting the bourgeois culture of leisure.[8] As a student at the Großherzoglich-Sächsische Kunstschule (Grand-Ducal Saxon Art School) in Weimar, Liebermann considered himself a figure painter and distanced himself from landscape painting.[9] It was not until later, in the 1890s, that he called himself a landscape painter.[10] On his honeymoon to Holland in 1884, the artist was already recording his impressions in sketching, including rare landscapes. On that trip Liebermann discovered many of his formative motifs, such as *Pig Market in Haarlem* (cats. 10, 11) and *Jewish Street in Amsterdam* (cat. 12). In *Pig Market in Haarlem (First Version)*, the artist's interest shifted from rich detail to the atmosphere of a day at the market characterized by sunshine. The soft, diffuse light begins to break up the forms. Shadowy areas alternate with bright reflections. An Impressionist flooding with light is already clearly recognizable here.

The Impressionist style of painting subsequently became established in several regional centers in Germany. In 1889 art critic Emil Heilbut gave a lecture at the Kunstschule in Weimar and showed three works by Claude Monet.[11] For many artists, including Christian Rohlfs, this was their first encounter with French Impressionism. The painter remarked on the works: "They caused a great sensation because of their colors and blotchy technique. . . . the bright colors were completely new to me."[12] In Weimar, Rohlfs discovered the striking motif of the Sternbrücke and the Kegelbrücke in close succession. Like Monet, he also painted how the appearance of the two bridges changed according to the time of day and the seasons. In the version of 1892, he concentrated entirely on the effects of light (cat. 20). The shimmering reflections beneath the balustrade are rendered in shades of red and white. Ludwig von Gleichen-Rußwurm, too, was left not unimpressed by Heilbut's lecture and tried to implement the new painting style (cat. 71). According to Julius Meier-Graefe in 1904, Gleichen-Rußwurm was the first German painter, "initially by himself, to introduce Impressionism into German painting."[13]

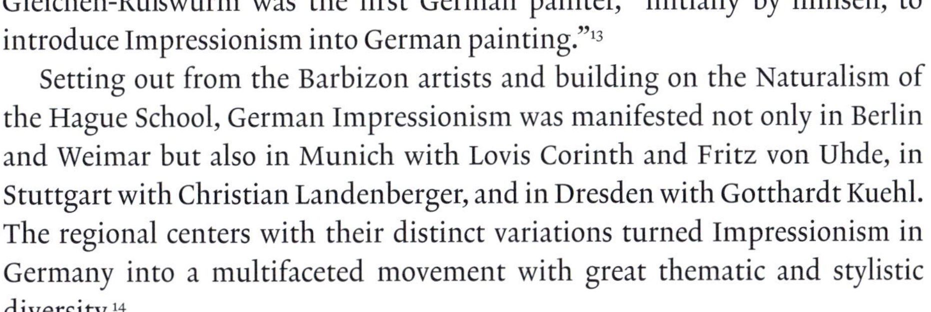

Setting out from the Barbizon artists and building on the Naturalism of the Hague School, German Impressionism was manifested not only in Berlin and Weimar but also in Munich with Lovis Corinth and Fritz von Uhde, in Stuttgart with Christian Landenberger, and in Dresden with Gotthardt Kuehl. The regional centers with their distinct variations turned Impressionism in Germany into a multifaceted movement with great thematic and stylistic diversity.[14]

Translated from German by Steven Lindberg

1

Max Liebermann (1847–1935)
Nursery—Pigpen, 1888
Private collection, Germany

2

Gotthardt Kuehl (1850–1915)
Northern German Hall with Woman Peeling Potatoes, 1885–90
Galerie von Negelein

3

Max Liebermann (1847–1935)
Tranquil Work, 1885
Museum Kunst der Westküste, Alkersum/Föhr

4

Fritz von Uhde (1848–1911)
Dutch Sewing Room, 1882
Private collection

5

Fritz von Uhde (1848–1911)
The Hurdy-Gurdy Man Is Coming, 1883
Hamburger Kunsthalle

6

Max Liebermann (1847–1935)
The Garden of the Amsterdam Orphanage, 1894
Musée d'Art moderne et contemporain de Strasbourg

7

Max Liebermann (1847–1935)
Free Period in the Amsterdam Orphanage, 1881–82
Städel Museum, Frankfurt am Main

8

Gotthardt Kuehl (1850–1915)
Lübeck Orphanage, 1894
Lübecker Museen. Museum Behnhaus Drägerhaus

9

Gotthardt Kuehl (1850–1915)
Orphans in Lübeck, 1884
Albertinum, Staatliche Kunstsammlungen Dresden

10

Max Liebermann (1847–1935)
Pig Market in Haarlem (First Version), 1890–91
Kunsthalle Mannheim

11

MAX LIEBERMANN (1847–1935)
Pig Market in Haarlem (Second Version), 1894
Hessisches Landesmuseum Darmstadt

12

Max Liebermann (1847–1935)
Jewish Street in Amsterdam, 1909
Private collection Brennet GmbH

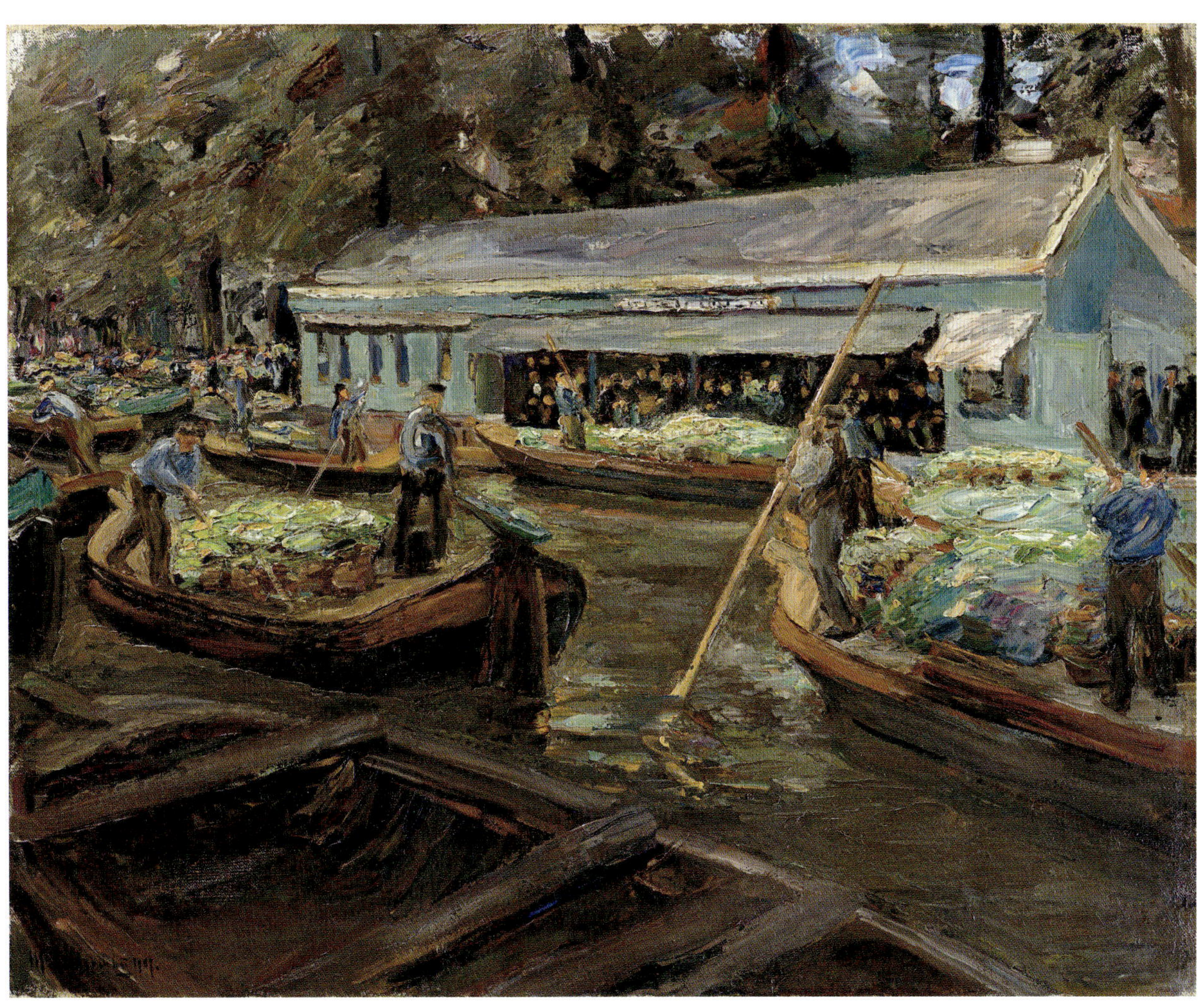

13

Max Liebermann (1847–1935)
Vegetable Market in Delft, 1907
Private collection, Berlin

14

Friedrich Kallmorgen (1856–1924)
Tableware Market, 1887
Kunsthalle Mannheim

15

Friedrich Kallmorgen (1856–1924)
Bright Winter Day, 1881
Private collection

16

Max Liebermann (1847–1935)
Saint Steven's Poorhouse in Leiden (Second Version), 1890
Private collection

17

Max Liebermann (1847–1935)
Hospital Garden in Edam, 1904
Belvedere, Vienna

18

Max Liebermann (1847–1935)
Harvest Field, 1912
Staatliche Kunsthalle Karlsruhe

19

Maria Slavona (1865–1931)
Landscape near the Oise, 1901–06
Lübecker Museen. Museum Behnhaus Drägerhaus

20

Christian Rohlfs (1849–1938)
The Sternbrücke in Weimar, 1892
Museum für Kunst und Kulturgeschichte Schloss Gottorf

21

Lovis Corinth (1858–1925)
Thriving Cottage Garden, 1904
Museum Wiesbaden

Valentina Plotnikova

Freshness and Dynamism

Out in the Open Air

The turn of the century brought with it a reorientation of German Impressionism. Artists discovered the culture of leisure as a new source for motifs. Searching for time to relax, far from the hubbub of the city, the bourgeoisie explored new activities such as riding outings and sailing trips. Impressionist landscapes alternated between promenades on the beach on the Dutch coastline and scenes of bathing in German lakes. Outdoor restaurants and beer gardens also joined the repertoire of motifs. These works reflect the desire of big-city dwellers to unwind outdoors.

The turn of the century marked a reorientation in the style and content of Impressionism in Germany. Artists discovered a new pictorial motif in middle-class leisure culture in nature close to the city. Many of them moved to the suburbs or took day trips to be closer to their subjects.[1]

Outdoor restaurants and beer gardens are seminal motifs in Max Liebermann's oeuvre. *Beer Garden in Brannenburg* (cat. 28) was painted almost entirely in the open air, and its bright colors and loose brushwork are typical of the start of his Impressionist phase. The atmosphere of a summer day is conveyed by bright puddles of light on the ground. Liebermann returned to this motif in Holland, his adopted home for painting. The thick crowns of trees permeated by spots of light in *De Oude Vink Beer Garden near Leiden* (cat. 26) seem like a recurring cipher in his Impressionist language, reappearing, for example, in *Beer Garden in Laren* (cat. 24) and *Colomierstrasse in Wannsee* (cat. 25).[2] Konrad von Kardorff also adopted this approach. His painting *Königin-Augusta-Strasse at Calandrelli-Platz in Berlin* (cat. 22) shows his artistic dialogue with Liebermann. The two were connected not only by the way they expressed themselves in painting but also by a close friendship. Von Kardorff was among those who paid their final respects at Liebermann's funeral.[3]

1
Pierre-Auguste Renoir, *La Grenouillère*, 1869, Nationalmuseum, Stockholm

After World War I broke out in 1914, artists had to search for motifs closer to home because trips abroad were scarcely possible. In outdoor restaurants on the Havel River, Liebermann found a wealth of new subjects (cats. 29, 30). The precursors of waterside inns as a subject were restaurants on the Seine outside of Paris—particularly La Grenouillère. Popular among rowboaters, it offered Impressionists such as Pierre-Auguste Renoir the ideal setting for depicting the play of colorful reflections of light on the water (fig. 1).

One new aspect of the bourgeois culture of leisure was walking—a social ritual in which seeing and being seen played an important role. While the lower classes walked by necessity, idle strolling was a sign of high social status.[4] Parks provided sites for contemplative retreat and invited quiet reflection.[5] The Tiergarten, which was near Liebermann's house on Pariser Platz in Berlin, was redesigned in the nineteenth century, transforming the royal hunting grounds into a public landscape park.[6] There, he produced numerous pictures of introspective flaneurs such as *Strollers in the Tiergarten* (cat. 23).

Excursions on horseback in the country were another popular leisure activity. In Liebermann's *Two Horsemen on the Road near Sakrow* (cat. 32) and Max Slevogt's *Group of Horsemen in the Forest* (cat. 31), the horses and riders seem to merge with their surroundings. The depiction of movement gives way to landscape. Riding is presented not as a social event but as a leisure activity in nature.

In the 1870s, the German bourgeoisie had discovered rowing and canoeing. A restaurant with a boat rental opened in 1872 on the former site of the Uhlenhorst ferry-house on the Outer Alster in Hamburg. In 1908 Alfred Lichtwark, director of the Hamburger Kunsthalle, invited Liebermann to paint a work for his "collection of paintings from Hamburg."[7] The artist chose an elevated standpoint from which he looked down on the landing pier in the basin. In the large sketch for the painting, the summer guests sitting at tables in the foreground are watching day-trippers on boats (cat. 35). Beneath a deep-blue sky, Liebermann showed a lively jumble of boats tacking.

Wannsee also offered new artistic inspirations. The rise in sailing coincided with Liebermann's purchase of a property next to the docks of the clubs, and he had his summer house built there.[8] Philipp Franck moved into a house on the Kleiner Wannsee. Inspired by the French Impressionists (fig. 2), he began to paint amateur sailors (cat. 42).

In the mid-nineteenth century, the culture of spa towns arose in Germany. The *Lebensreform* (Life Reform) movement propagated the healing qualities of water and contributed to swimming and sunbathing becoming established activities. Searching for recreation far from the bustle of the city, members of the high society discovered summer resorts by the sea. Guests strolled on the promenade by the shore or sat in wicker beach chairs. Initially a chic place for the upper-middle-class to retreat, the construction of the national railway system made the coast accessible to broader strata of the population.[9]

While the French Impressionists depicted the coasts of the Mediterranean or Normandy (fig. 3), the Germans found new motifs on the cooler beaches of the North and Baltic Seas. Liebermann's *After Bathing* (cat. 41) shows a group of boys enjoying themselves on the beach, far from social conventions. Following Liebermann, Franck also worked with his motif, shifting the action from the Dutch coast to the Stölpchensee, a lake to the south of Berlin. The picturesque fishing village of Stolpe inspired him to paint various views with playing children (cat. 43). Christian Landenberger, whose painting sojourns took him to Lake Constance and the Ammersee in southern Germany, depicted young people outdoors. In *Summer Evening at the Lake* (cat. 36), he combined realistic figure painting with Impressionist effects of light.

In 1900 Liebermann, himself a passionate rider, turned his eyes to summer vacationers on horseback (cats. 33, 34). In the 1903 version, the lady, in accordance with etiquette, wears a skirt and a small man's hat and holds a pretty riding crop. Riding was one of the few athletic activities open to women. For them, however, it was more about social exchange and aesthetics: "A lady should ride well and elegantly, or else not at all."[10]

Liebermann's depictions of the beach at Noordwijk in Holland focus less on the summer vacationers in the foreground than on the light-flooded atmosphere of a pleasant day by the sea (cats. 39, 40). With a few brushstrokes, the artist suggested the silhouettes only sketchily. The accents of color of the clothing and flags stand out against the bright beach shimmering in the sunlight and structure the composition. In *On the Baltic Shore* (cat. 38), Lovis Corinth took a different approach and shifted the focus to the protagonist: Charlotte Berend, his student and later wife. This portrait of her standing on the dunes in a long, white dress was painted the year the couple became engaged.

German Impressionists combined the atmospheric charm of nature with leisure activities in their paintings, turning artists into chroniclers of modern leisure entertainments. Their works reflect the yearning of city people for recreation outdoors.

Translated from German by Steven Lindberg

2
Pierre-Auguste Renoir,
The Seine at Argenteuil, 1874,
Portland Art Museum

3
Claude Monet,
The Beach at Trouville, 1870,
Wadsworth Atheneum Museum of Art, Hartford

22

Konrad von Kardorff (1877–1945)
Königin-Augusta-Strasse at Calandrelli-Platz in Berlin, 1911
Stiftung Stadtmuseum Berlin

23

Max Liebermann (1847–1935)
Strollers in the Tiergarten, ca. 1927
Private collection

24

MAX LIEBERMANN (1847–1935)
Beer Garden in Laren, 1903
Private collection

25

Max Liebermann (1847–1935)
Colomierstrasse in Wannsee, 1917
Private collection

26

MAX LIEBERMANN (1847–1935)
De Oude Vink Beer Garden near Leiden, 1905
Kunsthaus Zürich

27

Max Uth (1863–1914)
The Beer Garden, ca. 1910
Staatliche Museen zu Berlin, Nationalgalerie

28

Max Liebermann (1847–1935)
Beer Garden in Brannenburg, 1893
Musée d'Orsay, Paris

29

Max Liebermann (1847–1935)
Beer Garden on the Havel Under the Trees, 1920–22
Private collection

30

Max Liebermann (1847–1935)
Beer Garden on the Havel Under the Trees, 1920–22
Private collection

31

Max Slevogt (1868–1932)
Group of Horsemen in the Forest, 1902
Private collection

32

Max Liebermann (1847–1935)
Two Horsemen on the Road near Sakrow, 1924
Galerie Bastian, Berlin

33

Max Liebermann (1847–1935)
Horseman and Horsewoman on the Beach, 1903
Wallraf-Richartz-Museum & Fondation Corboud, Cologne

34

Max Liebermann (1847–1935)
Two Horsemen on the Beach Facing Left, ca. 1910
Museum Kunst der Westküste, Alkersum/Föhr

35

MAX LIEBERMANN (1847–1935)
Summer Evening on the Alster, 1909
Leopold-Hoesch-Museum, Düren

36

Christian Landenberger (1862–1927)
Summer Evening at the Lake, 1904
Bayerische Staatsgemäldesammlungen, Munich—Neue Pinakothek

37

Max Liebermann (1847–1935)
Beach Life, 1916
Private collection

38

Lovis Corinth (1858–1925)
On the Baltic Shore, 1903
Private collection

39

Max Liebermann (1847–1935)
On the Beach at Noordwijk, 1908
Von der Heydt-Museum Wuppertal

40

Max Liebermann (1847–1935)
On the Beach at Noordwijk, 1908
Staatliche Kunsthalle Karlsruhe

41

Max Liebermann (1847–1935)
After Bathing, 1904
Tate, London

42

Philipp Franck (1860–1944)
Wannsee, 1915
Private collection, Frankfurt am Main

43

Philipp Franck (1860–1944)
Boys Swimming, 1911
Private collection

Valentina Plotnikova

An Eye on Modernity

Cityscapes

Urban renewal from 1862 onward transformed Berlin into a modern metropolis. Broad boulevards and artificial lighting made the streets and the night worth depicting. In a dialogue with French views of the city, Impressionists in Germany developed their own visual idiom. Their themes were social tensions such as the anonymity of life in big cities. Enthusiasm about progress met with gloomy visions of urbanization. Painters revealed an ambivalent view of the metropolis between dynamic cultural space and a place of emotional stress. They were already anticipating Expressionist themes.

The urban renewal of Paris under Baron Haussmann from the 1850s onward established a new type for the metropolis. Berlin, the capital of Prussia, followed this classic example of modern urbanization with the Hobrecht Plan of 1862. Its layout with broad sidewalks and boulevards with trees led to the conquest of the street by the curious flaneur roaming the city.[1] Then the night was conquered with modern gas and electric lighting. The day was extended into the night; nocturnal cafés were conducive to social life (cats. 56, 60). The zeitgeist was epitomized by Café Bauer, which was the first to have electric lighting and remain open around the clock.[2]

This conquest of the night and of the street inspired artists to explore urban space visually. The French Impressionists developed a composition with a boulevard captured in excerpts that became the type that defined the cityscape. Édouard Manet implemented it in *The Rue Mosnier with Flags,* which shows the view from his studio in Paris during the Festival of Peace and Work (fig. 1). Max Slevogt, who owned the work, responded with *Unter den Linden (Flags in Berlin)* (cat. 47), in which he depicted the twenty-fifth anniversary of the reign of Emperor Wilhelm II. The military parade has been rendered in rapid brushstrokes: soldiers, viewers, trees, and pavement merge into a dynamic plane of colors.

1
Édouard Manet,
The Rue Mosnier with Flags, 1878,
private collection

2
Camille Pissarro,
The Boulevard Montmartre at Night, 1897,
National Gallery, London

Lovis Corinth oriented *Unter den Linden* (cat. 51) around Camille Pissarro, who had painted the Boulevard Montmartre from an elevated viewpoint (fig. 2). With a similar perspective from an upper floor, Corinth offered a diagonal view of Berlin's stately boulevard—but that is where the similarities end. The distorted renderings of buildings tipped to the side undermine any possible ordering of the composition. In contrast to the bright colors of French Impressionism, Corinth made use of dull colors and cool shades, creating a somber atmosphere. In 1920 the painter wrote, "In the meantime, let us see Berlin as it is today, entirely intact and untouched by all the destruction to come."[3] The painting's reproduction of the tension dominating the metropolis connects it stylistically to Expressionism.

Depictions of Neuer See, whose beer garden and boat rentals made it a popular weekend destination in Berlin, also illustrate the ambiguity of German Impressionism. Gustave Caillebotte's celebration of the modern approach to leisure time, with animated rowers on a sunny day (fig. 3), contrasts clearly with Corinth's artistic vision. For *Neuer See in the Tiergarten in Berlin* (cat. 44), he chose a cloudy day when the boathouse remained closed. The sky flashing between the trunks of trees seems murky. In muted colors, Corinth shows a landscape void of people. His interest focused not on weekend pleasures in the city but on its silent backdrops. In *Ice Rink in the Tiergarten in Berlin* (cat. 46), Corinth took up this motif again, now animated by ice skaters. Liebermann chose a similar theme in *Ice Skaters in the Tiergarten* (cat. 45), in which he showed the movement of a vibrant crowd of small figures under wan light. The artist developed his clearly bright motifs in zoos. A work produced in Amsterdam's zoo, *Parrot Man* (cat. 48), is characterized by a bright palette of brilliant blue, red, and yellow. Liebermann depicted a peaceful afternoon with cheery colors on which the city and its people come together in harmonious unity.

While the evolution of the metropolis was seen positively in France, despite some criticism, Germany was dominated by an attitude that often rejected it. Oswald Spengler expressed this in 1922 in his book *Der Untergang des Abendlandes* (translated as *The Decline of the West*). Spengler saw urbanization as a symptom of civilization's decline.[4] The German Impressionists responded to society's skepticism. In their works, the city is a space of contradictory experiences: both a dynamic cultural space and a symbol of industrial process, distanced surroundings, and a place of alienation. The people often look like staffage figures, lost in the anonymous crowd. This anonymity as a new aspect of metropolitan life is also reflected in the "unknown passerby" of Charles Baudelaire.[5] The recurring sketchy figure of a woman in the work of Lesser Ury—for example, *Carriages (Rainy Atmosphere)* (cat. 58), *Nocturnal Street Scene, Berlin* (cat. 59), and *Bellevuestrasse, Berlin* (cat. 54)—embodies the isolation of city dwellers.

At the end of the nineteenth century, neurologists were studying the psychological ailments of people living in large cities.[6] In the public debate, the concept of nervousness gained acceptance and was associated with the hectic life in the metropolis. In his cityscapes, Ury dramatized artificial light—whether from streetlamps or the headlights of cabs and cars—as a symbol of growing nervousness. He was conveying the dynamism but also the drama of urban life, where people were suffering from time pressures and the accelerated tempo of life.

While the French Impressionists tended to depict artificial lighting as a passive element in street scenes (fig. 2), Ury gave light an active role. In *Elevated Subway Station at Bülowstrasse* (cat. 57), the vibrating traces of headlights run through the scene as a central element of the painting. The lights and their reflections on the wet street condense into a symbol of the nervous tension of the metropolis. The silhouettes of vehicles are almost extinguished by the intense light. The light is materialized and functions as a mediator but also a trigger of urban nervousness. It becomes an autonomous protagonist of the action in the painting.

Unlike the colorful palette of the French Impressionists, Ury's works are limited to a few colors. He depicts the light source in a reduced palette of shades of white, yellow, and orange, for example, in *Nocturnal Street Scene, Berlin* (cat. 59). The light is not naturalistic but intensified, dominating the cityscape with its intense radiance, as in *Café König at Night (Unter den Linden)* (cat. 56).

In the twentieth century, German artists faced other challenges than their precursors had. While the French Impressionists discovered the metropolis as an aesthetic phenomenon, German artists wanted to convey the inner, emotional world of the city dweller. The Impressionist painting of Germany therefore already has features of later Expressionism in that the artists interpreted the city as the scene of existential conflicts. In their cityscapes they portrayed the social features of modern life such as the anonymity of the metropolis or the nervousness of the modern generation.

Translated from German by Steven Lindberg

3
Gustave Caillebotte,
Skiffs, 1877,
National Gallery of Art, Washington

44

Lovis Corinth (1858–1925)
Neuer See in the Tiergarten in Berlin, 1903
Kunsthalle Mannheim

45

Max Liebermann (1847–1935)
Ice Skaters in the Tiergarten, 1921
Private collection, Berlin

46

Lovis Corinth (1858–1925)
Ice Rink in the Tiergarten in Berlin, 1909
Hegenbarth Collection Berlin

47

Max Slevogt (1868–1932)
Unter den Linden (Flags in Berlin), 1913
Hessisches Landesmuseum Darmstadt

48

Max Liebermann (1847–1935)
Parrot Man, 1901
Private collection

49

Eva Stort (1855–1936)
View from the Window (Schöneberg), 1890
David Ragusa Collection

50

Lovis Corinth (1858–1925)
Garden in Berlin-Westend, 1925
Von der Heydt-Museum Wuppertal

51

Lovis Corinth (1858–1925)
Unter den Linden, 1922
Von der Heydt-Museum Wuppertal

52

Gotthardt Kuehl (1850–1915)
View of Dresden with the Augustus Bridge at Night, ca. 1900
Kunstforum Ostdeutsche Galerie, Regensburg

53

Lesser Ury (1861–1931)
Street at Night in the Rain (Berlin), ca. 1898–1900
Private collection

54

LESSER URY (1861–1931)
Bellevuestrasse, Berlin, 1912
Private collection

55

Lesser Ury (1861–1931)
Nocturnal Street Scene, Berlin—Leipziger Strasse, ca. 1915–20
Private collection

56

Lesser Ury (1861–1931)
Café König at Night (Unter den Linden), 1925–30
Private collection, southern Germany

57

Lesser Ury (1861–1931)
Elevated Subway Station at Bülowstrasse, 1922
Private collection, southern Germany

58

Lesser Ury (1861–1931)
Carriages (Rainy Atmosphere), 1916
Private collection

59

Lesser Ury (1861–1931)
Nocturnal Street Scene, Berlin, ca. 1915–20
Dr. Matthias Wilkening Foundation

60

Lesser Ury (1861–1931)
Woman and Man in a Café, 1920s
Private collection

61

Lesser Ury (1861–1931)
Woman and Man, Unter den Linden, 1889
Private collection, southern Germany

62

Max Liebermann (1847–1935)
Concert at the Opera, 1922
Arp Museum Bahnhof Rolandseck, Remagen, courtesy private collection, Cologne

63

Lesser Ury (1861–1931)
Café de la Paix at Night, Paris, 1928
Private collection, southern Germany

Daniel Zamani

Intimate Worlds

Houses and Gardens

As it was in France, Impressionism in Germany was an art of the bourgeoisie. Although numerous paintings show the conquest of public space, the Impressionists were also committed to depicting houses and gardens. Their insights into family life alternate between intimate scenes and striving for representation. They share a focus on the home as a haven that is connected to closeness and to the development of one's own reality. They often function as ideal images that invite identification while also reflecting the experiential world of the bourgeoisie.

In his unfinished *Passagen-Werk* (translated as *Arcades Project*, 1927–40), philosopher and sociologist Walter Benjamin described the nineteenth century as "addicted to dwelling."[1] The rapid rise of the bourgeoisie was also accompanied by a retreat into the private that attributed great importance to one's own home and garden. Early on, the French Impressionists recognized the potential for this new, financially powerful class of buyers to become their patrons and successfully mobilized it for their own ends. In their works, they turned away from large-format depictions of historical and religious themes and instead explored motifs that concerned the lives and experiences of the bourgeoisie or deliberately provided ideal images with which the buyers liked to decorate their private interiors. Their views of gardens and depictions of their own homes overwhelmingly convey an impression of carefree calm and harmony—a focus on intimacy that invited viewers to identify with it and that would also become typical of the pictorial worlds of German Impressionists (see figs. 1, 2).

1
Mary Cassatt,
The Child's Bath, 1893,
Art Institute of Chicago

Scenes of joyful family life play a prominent role in the oeuvre of Lovis Corinth, who together with Max Liebermann and Max Slevogt formed the so-called triumvirate of German Impressionism. In 1904 Corinth married his student Charlotte Berend, who modeled for numerous interiors and figure paintings and was herself a successful artist (see cat. 88). In 1900 they moved into a grand three-story apartment in Berlin's Hansaviertel and elegantly decorated its rooms. Over four days of sittings in 1911, Corinth painted *Woman at the Goldfish Tank* (cat. 66). Charlotte Berend-Corinth wears a striped velvet dress and has retired to a cozy, plant-filled bay window to read. Corinth rendered details such as the many goldfish swimming around and the splendor of flowers in the background in luminous colors, and the entire interior is animated by a complex play of flickers of sunlight.

The aspect of marital idyll is brought to bear even more forcefully in the work *Morning Sun* (cat. 65), in which Charlotte Berend-Corinth is seen in a reclining pose, smiling invitingly at the viewer. Pillows, sheets, and her airy, light dress in delicate gradations of white and gray form a frame that effectively brings out the flesh tones of her body. The sketch-like rendering of the objects and the tight framing convey the impression of a snapshot—as if the artist were offering the viewer an unvarnished view into his bedroom at home, seemingly in passing.

The bourgeois home as a site of artistic research is also an important topos in the late works of Max Slevogt, who had moved from Munich to the German capital in 1901. The painting *House in Godramstein—Wolfgang with Goat* (cat. 79) is reminiscent of the many paintings by Claude Monet in which he lovingly portrayed his elder son, Jean, in the middle of the family garden filled with sunlight. On the left, Slevogt shows the imposing Neoclassical country home that his father-in-law had built in Godramstein in the Palatinate. From 1909 to 1913, Slevogt and his family regularly spent the summer months in this *Schlössl*, or "little castle," which offered them a welcome refuge from the hectic bustle of the metropolis. Here, his small son, Wolfgang, is enjoying playing with a goat, flanked on the right by lush foliage whose rich shades of green underscore the impression of the freshness of summer. Like the stylistically closely related *Children at the Pond* (cat. 76) or *Garden Path to the Summer House (Godramstein)* (cat. 74), the lively brushwork and luminous colors here testify to the influence of Édouard Manet, whose depictions of nature Slevogt would have studied in exhibitions at Paul Cassirer's Kunstsalon in Berlin, among other places.

Regarding one's own surroundings as worthy of painting and the intention to depict interiors in a natural way are also features of numerous German Impressionist works depicting the children of the artists or of their patrons with pride and dignity (see cats. 80–82, 84–91)—often in the effective scenery of cheery, light-flooded interiors (see cats. 87, 91).[2] One of the women painters of children's portraits in Germany during the Weimar Republic who was most in demand was Sabine Lepsius, who with her colleague Dora Hitz was one of the few female founding members of the Berlin Secession. For her double portrait of sisters Cornelia and Charlotte Hahn (see cat. 91), Lepsius chose the cactus window of their parents' conservatory as a background—presumably as an indirect reference to the mother of the sitters, Beate Hahn, who wrote garden books for children and whose garden was designed by famous landscape architect Karl Foerster. The girls are standing close together, and their identical clothing—white blouses with red embroidered decorations—artfully conveys the sister's bond.

The importance of his own home is reflected in Max Liebermann's oeuvre above all by nearly two hundred paintings dedicated to his summer home on the Wannsee and its reformist garden—spacious grounds on whose design he had consulted art historian Alfred Lichtwark.[3] In particular, compositions in which the garden is animated by family members such as Liebermann's grandchild, Maria (the child of his only daughter, Käthe), reflect a view of the house on the Wannsee as the epitome of refuge (see cats. 117, 125, 127). Even more so than other pioneers of German modernism, including Slevogt and Corinth, Liebermann was a prominent figure in the intense culture wars to which the avant-garde was exposed in the politically divided Weimar Republic. At the same time, after World War I began, the painter was increasingly disturbed by growing antisemitic hostilities and the continuing criticism of the deliberate internationality for which the German Impressionists had courageously fought since the 1880s. Depicting his secluded garden by the Wannsee as a carefree idyll reflects in Liebermann's case the literally existential significance of a protected place. After the transition of power to the Nazis, the painter anticipated the new regime by resigning from his position as honorary president of the Prussian Academy of the Arts.

Translated from German by Steven Lindberg

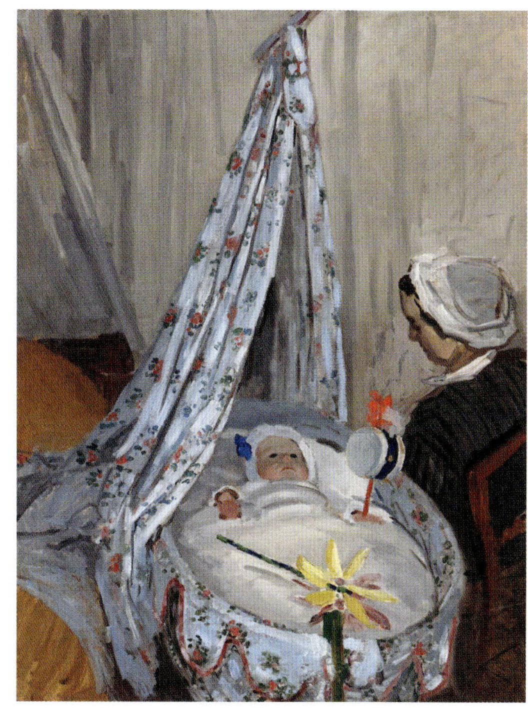

2
Claude Monet,
The Cradle—Camille with the Artist's Son Jean, 1867,
National Gallery of Art, Washington

64

Lovis Corinth (1858–1925)
Woman Reading, 1911
Private collection

65

Lovis Corinth (1858–1925)
Morning Sun, 1910
Hessisches Landesmuseum Darmstadt

66

Lovis Corinth (1858–1925)
Woman at the Goldfish Tank, 1911
Belvedere, Vienna

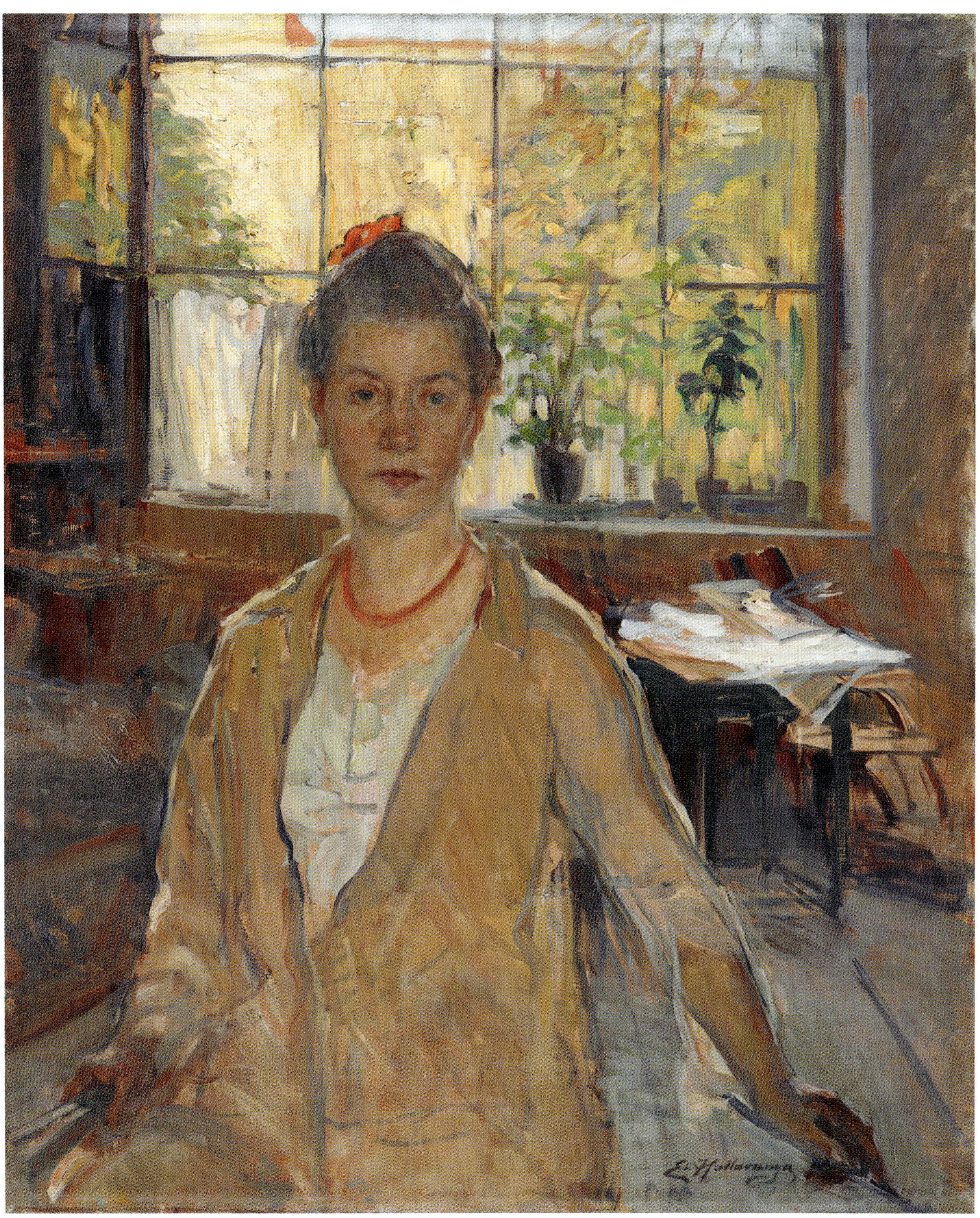

67

Emilie von Hallavanya (1874–1960)
Self-Portrait, 1905 (?)
Städtische Galerie im Lenbachhaus und Kunstbau, Munich

68

Lovis Corinth (1858–1925)
Christmas Tree (Distributing Presents), 1913
Lentos Kunstmuseum Linz

69

Franz Skarbina (1849–1910)
Christmas Room, Berlin, 1892
Stiftung Stadtmuseum Berlin

70

Wilhelm Trübner (1851–1917)
Girl in a Tree, 1907
Kurpfälzisches Museum Heidelberg

71

Ludwig von Gleichen-Russwurm (1836–1901)
Stroll Under Flowering Apple Trees, 1893
Museum im Kulturspeicher, Würzburg

72

PHILIPP FRANCK (1860–1944)
Wannsee Garden (Rose Arbor in the Arnholds' Garden), 1919
Private collection

73

Lovis Corinth (1858–1925)
Flowering Apple Tree, 1922
Private collection

74

Max Slevogt (1868–1932)
Garden Path to the Summer House (Godramstein), 1912
Private collection

75

Max Slevogt (1868–1932)
The Hollyhock Gardener, 1920
Kunsthalle Mannheim

76

Max Slevogt (1868–1932)
Children at the Pond (Garden in Godramstein), 1909
Private collection

77

Max Slevogt (1868–1932)
Gardener in Front of the House, 1910
Private collection

78

Max Slevogt (1868–1932)
Bathing Boys, 1911
Belvedere, Vienna

79

Max Slevogt (1868–1932)
House in Godramstein—Wolfgang with Goat, 1909
Private collection

Ortrud Westheider

Full of Expectation

Paintings of Children

In the late nineteenth century, the children of the people responsible for the economic boom in Germany, known as the *Gründerzeit,* or "founders' era," were captured in portraits. They were modeled on the paintings of children by Pierre-Auguste Renoir and Mary Cassatt that were commissioned by French and American patrons who were also founding bourgeois dynasties. They had great expectations of their offspring and invested a great deal of care in their education. Sunlight and the free style of Impressionist painting also express the children's lack of inhibition and the spirit of a new beginning. In this way, these paintings testify to an impulse for freedom in reform pedagogy.

In the "century of the child,"[1] the little ones conquered the world of the adults. Paintings around 1900 show them with toys in living rooms. One child has created her own space by setting up an accordion-folded book like a ring fortress (cat. 80). With miniature houses at her feet, another girl holds a church in her hand, which hangs down in a relaxed gesture, and gazes at the viewer (cat. 82). It is uncertain whether she will carefully position the toy church as the finishing touch to the scene under construction or if she will throw it on the floor to prompt a new game.

The paintings of the German Impressionists illustrate the change in relationships between the generations around 1900. A book by Swedish women's rights advocate Ellen Key was a bestseller in the German Empire. Unlike Clara Zetkin, who focused on the children of the working classes in her contemporaneous writings on reform pedagogy, Key examined the relationship of the bourgeois parent and child. By criticizing the alliance of clericalism and militarism, she called for a responsible approach to the next generation in the new century. Key formulated apodictic ideas of a "holiness of the child" in which nature perfects itself. With her critique of corporal punishment and the teaching of religion and her vision of transforming schools from places of education to places of inspiration to counter what she called "soul murder," she was challenging the reform movements of industrial societies and providing new inspiration to artists as well.[2]

1
Pierre-Auguste Renoir,
The Children's Afternoon in Wargemont, 1884,
Alte Nationalgalerie, Berlin

2
John Singer Sargent,
Ruth Sears Bacon, 1887,
Wadsworth Atheneum Museum of Art, Hartford

In Fritz von Uhde's painting *Children's Room* (cat. 87), the children appear free and unobserved.[3] They are pursuing their own ideas in a room flooded by sunlight. As in Max Liebermann's *Nursery School in Amsterdam* (1880, Alte Nationalgalerie, Berlin), the nanny is focused on her knitting, allowing her young charges to play freely with their dolls. The playing children have marveled at the miniature houses and trees on the floor and spun them around, but also neglectfully dismissed them. The parquet floor gleaming in the sunlight makes the interior seem as if painted *en plein air* and emphasizes the unrestrained and animated nature of the children's activity with their dolls. It draws the world into this small scene and incorporates everything the girls think up. Open shoes, socks slipped down, and a towel hanging to dry over the small bed testify to free, unregulated time and an informal space that encourages self-initiated learning. Uhde supplemented the children's play by giving the dolls lives of their own: they gaze out the open window at the neighbors, look at the window-panes across the way, or watch the children playing from the lower end of the table or from the carriage.

Children's games included dressing up and role-playing. In 1907 Max Slevogt proposed to Paul Cassirer an illustrated edition of a German translation of the *Leatherstocking Tales.*[4] The artist's children inspired his interest in James Fenimore Cooper's book for young people. In 1909 it was published with more than three hundred lithographs by Slevogt. In 1913 he painted his son, Wolfgang (Landesmuseum, Mainz), and his daughter, Nina (cat. 81), decked out in feathers and leather fringes. Their surroundings, rendered sketchily in earth tones, underscore a wish to make naturalness a theme of this painting of children. The story of ranger Natty Bumppo and his friendship with a Mohican takes place at a time when Indigenous Americans were being displaced and persecuted. In colonialist Germany, the book offered an opportunity to identify with the victims of progress.

Although an artist's own children might be impatient models, they were close at hand in daily life. Presented in a sequined silk dress in front of a commode with Rococo fittings (cat. 86), however, they might attract the attention of a well-heeled clientele of buyers. The girl's gold bracelet and pearls on her wrists and ankles suggests that she is the scion of a wealthy family. Sabine Lepsius painted her daughter with her loose hair tied on the side with a ribbon and her legs crossed on a shining blue cloth on the floor. The sunlight and her pose make it look like a scene in the open air. Lepsius saw the Impressionist painting style as an opportunity to capture the child model on canvas in a situation, "like a bird spotted and painted in flight."[5] Pierre-Auguste Renoir had won over the bourgeoisie of Paris with paintings of children in the 1880s and received numerous commissions for portraits (fig. 1), and John Singer Sargent also offered his services to potential American collectors of the Gilded Age with portraits of children (fig. 2).[6]

Recourse to famous precursors was widespread in the genre of child portraits. For example, in his *Portrait of a Child* (1862, Kunsthalle Karlsruhe), Édouard Manet alluded to Diego Velázquez. Sabine Lepsius oriented her formal portrait of Margarete Catharina Litten (cat. 85) on James McNeil Whistler's painting *Symphony in White, No. 1: The White Girl* (fig. 3), a work that had been widely reproduced since the World's Fair in Paris in 1867. Like Whistler, Lepsius placed the girl in a white dress in front of white curtains.

Women Impressionists such as Mary Cassatt, Eva Gonzalès, and Berthe Morisot had turned the portrait of a child into a genre for women. Their models were their own children and nieces and nephews as well as the children of friends. Charlotte Berend-Corinth, a student, model, and from 1904 wife of Lovis Corinth, exhibited at the Berlin Secession in 1906. One year earlier, she had portrayed Henriette Seckbach (cat. 88). Blue bows decorate her clothing and hair, as does a bouquet of violet anemones. The girl still has to grow into her dress, and her role as Flora, the goddess of spring, is far in the future. The dress that has slipped down and the bows recall Andrea della Robbia's *Infants in Swaddling Clothes* from 1487 at the Ospedale degli Innocenti in Florence.

Dora Hitz came from Paris to Berlin, where she founded a painting school for women in 1894 and specialized in Impressionist portraits of the liberal bourgeoisie.[7] She shows the girl at eye level, making her seem majestic on a chair that is too large for her small form (cat. 89). Only her freely falling gold-blond locks distinguish this portrait from one of an adult. The fashionable black ribbon in her hair corresponds to the red flowers of the wallpaper. The triad of black, white, and red reflects the colors of the German Empire, possibly a reference to the future role of the young generation in society.

Translated from German by Steven Lindberg

3
James McNeill Whistler,
Symphony in White, No. 1: The White Girl, 1861–63/1872,
National Gallery of Art, Washington

80

Max Slevogt (1868–1932)
Portrait of Suzanne Aimée Cassirer, 1901
Private collection

81

MAX SLEVOGT (1868–1932)
Nina as an Indian, 1913
Landesmuseum Mainz

82

Heinrich Eduard Linde-Walther (1868–1939)
Child in a Playroom, 1901
Lübecker Museen. Museum Behnhaus Drägerhaus

83

Fritz von Uhde (1848–1911)
The Garden Path, 1903
Kunsthalle Bremen—Der Kunstverein in Bremen

84

Fritz von Uhde (1848–1911)
The Lesson, 1899
Museum Folkwang, Essen

85

Sabine Lepsius (1864–1942)
Portrait of a Child (Margarete Catharina Litten), 1895
Staatliche Museen zu Berlin, Nationalgalerie

86

Sabine Lepsius (1864–1942)
Monica, the Artist's Daughter, 1900
Staatliche Museen zu Berlin, Nationalgalerie

87

Fritz von Uhde (1848–1911)
Children's Room, 1889
Hamburger Kunsthalle

88

Charlotte Berend-Corinth (1880–1967)
Henny (Henriette Seckbach), 1905
Städtische Galerie im Lenbachhaus und Kunstbau, Munich

89

Dora Hitz (1856–1924)
Portrait of a Small Girl, before 1897
Staatliche Museen zu Berlin, Nationalgalerie

90

Sabine Lepsius (1864–1942)
Girl in Sunday Dress, 1914
David Ragusa Collection

91

Sabine Lepsius (1864–1942)
Double Portrait of the Sisters Cornelia (Born in 1921) and Charlotte Hahn (Born in 1926), 1932
Jüdisches Museum Berlin

Daniel Zamani

The Liberation of Color

Still Life

As an independent pictorial genre, still life developed in the Netherlands of the seventeenth century. There, the decorative arrangement of widely varying objects was governed not only by aesthetic considerations but also by symbolic associations. Avant-garde artists of the nineteenth century banished this allegorizing dimension from their still lifes and instead adopted the genre as an experimental arena for painterly innovation. The still lifes of the German Impressionists are also characterized by the liberation of color as an autonomous aesthetic element. The energetic brushwork and sketch-like articulation of the surface often lend the works a strikingly abstract character.

From the earliest phase of the movement, the genre of still life played an important role in the development of French Impressionism. Artists such as Édouard Manet, Claude Monet, and later Gustave Caillebotte used it to explore painterly problems such as the representation of spatial depth, the play of shadow and light, and the rendering of various textures. Among the first works of modern French art to enter the collection of the Nationalgalerie in Berlin was Manet's *White Lilacs* (fig. p. 33) from around 1882, part of a group of late still lifes that the artist had painted shortly before his death and that were highly esteemed by both Hugo von Tschudi and Max Liebermann. The painting had belonged to husband-and-wife collectors Carl and Felicie Bernstein since 1882 and was bequeathed to the museum in Berlin after Felicie Bernstein's death in 1908. Liebermann, who admired Manet the most of all his French colleagues, acquired two of Manet's late floral still lifes for his own collection: *Crystal Vase with Roses, Tulips, and White Lilac* (ca. 1881, private collection) and *Peonies* (fig. p. 61).[1] In 1922 the painting in the Nationalgalerie served as a source of inspiration for a still life by Lesser Ury entitled *Bouquet of Lilacs* (cat. 102). Although Ury chose a significantly larger format, like Manet he too presents a closely cropped view of the motif in which the white flowers, suggested in thick, impasto strokes, seem to glow against a dark background.

1
Claude Monet,
Still Life with Spanish Melon, 1879,
Hasso Plattner Collection,
Museum Barberini, Potsdam

While Ury's bouquet is largely isolated from its spatial context, Heinrich Hübner situated his *Larkspurs* (cat. 103) at the threshold between still life and interior. Hübner had joined the Berlin Secession in 1902 and produced numerous paintings in the early years of the twentieth century in which he emulated the colorism of the French Impressionists. Here he shows a cropped view of a table and a green garden bench on a loggia in the summertime. The focal point of the composition is a magnificent bouquet of blue and white larkspurs in a bright blue stoneware pitcher. On the table to the right of the pitcher is a silver tray with a white porcelain plate and a crystal bowl containing a yellow melon. The stone balustrade of the loggia, entwined with creeping vines from the outside, is rendered in light pastel hues of blue and pink. With a fascination for detail, Hübner captured the reflections of light on the varying materials of stone, crystal, and porcelain and even suggested the colored shadows on the tabletop—a striving for the authentic rendering of optical sensations already characteristic of French Impressionism.

The still lifes of Maria Slavona, who spent many years in the French capital from 1890 on, similarly show the influence of the Parisian avant-garde. In France, Slavona discovered Impressionism and Post-Impressionism and was fascinated by the brilliantly colored pictorial vision of Vincent van Gogh, of whose works she herself owned several. In *Still Life with Red Background* (cat. 95), the artist presents a table adorned with a white and red cloth on which fruits and flowers are carefully arranged. The closely cropped composition is executed entirely in vivid colors, with powerful accents of green, yellow, and violet contrasting with the dominant crimson red. Slavona participated in the hotly contested Paris exhibition scene by showing at the Salon d'Automne as well as the Salon des Indépendants and was able to build bridges to the French avant-garde early on through connections such as her friendship with Camille Pissarro. In 1913 she moved to Berlin, where shortly after her death in 1931, the Nationalgalerie honored her with a major special exhibition at the venerable Kronprinzenpalais.

As with Slavona, the influence of France also comes to expression in the late works of Max Slevogt. The painting *Red Carnations* from 1904 (cat. 94) recalls the flower still lifes of Gustave Caillebotte (fig. 2). Here the differentiated handling of the paint and the luminous color produce a remarkable sense of dynamism within a small pictorial space. The tactile modeling of the carnations, standing out in fiery tones against the dark brown background, gives them an almost sculptural effect, while a deeper shade of red appears in the pattern of the tablecloth, which is rendered more flatly than the opulent, impasto flowers. The bright white envelope and folded sheet of paper on the right set a pronounced accent that enriches the composition with a narrative element. Slevogt's affinity with French Impressionism shows itself even more clearly in his *Still Life with Chocolate Rabbits* from 1923 (cat. 92), which bears a remarkable resemblance to the still lifes of Monet. The open treatment of the surface and the energetic brushwork enhance the appeal of the Easter-themed motif. Slevogt depicted a bright red tablecloth on which a variety of treats—Easter eggs, chocolate rabbits, and fancy cakes—are decoratively arranged. In the still life *Summer Flowers* from five years later (cat. 93), the painter likewise embraced a sketch-like approach to the pictorial elements as well as a fresh color scheme—borrowings from modern French art that also characterize his late Impressionist landscapes (see cats. 74–79).

The liberation of color from its mimetic purposes is strikingly manifested in the many expressive paintings produced by Lovis Corinth during the final years before his death in 1925. In *Flower Still Life (Calla Lilies and Lilacs with Bronze Figure)* (cat. 101), the artist used a spirited wet-in-wet technique to capture the pictorial objects. On the pulsating surface of the canvas, the individual elements are scarcely perceptible as solid, independent forms. The arrangement of amaryllis and lilac includes the favorite flowers of Corinth's wife, Charlotte, complemented by a small blue vase with lilies of the valley and a flower bowl whose contents dissolve into a play of luminous color. The areas rendered with painterly gusto in broad strokes of the brush effectively contrast with the striking silhouette of the bronze figure in black; positioned in the right half of the picture, it provides a stabilizing counterweight to the swelling form of the Meissen vase with its opulent floral splendor. In a manner typical of German Impressionist still lifes, Corinth here skillfully combines the free play of color and form with a cool gaze for compositional balance.

Translated from German by Melissa M. Thorson

2
Gustave Caillebotte,
Lilacs and Peonies in Two Vases, 1883,
Hasso Plattner Collection,
Museum Barberini, Potsdam

92

Max Slevogt (1868–1932)
Still Life with Chocolate Rabbits, 1923
Landesmuseum Mainz

93

Max Slevogt (1868–1932)
Summer Flowers, 1928
Private collection, courtesy Daxer & Marschall, Munich

94

Max Slevogt (1868–1932)
Red Carnations, 1904
Private collection

95

Maria Slavona (1865–1931)
Still Life with Red Background, 1911
Stiftung Schlösschen im Hofgarten Wertheim

96

Georg Burmester (1864–1936)
Bouquet of Summer Flowers, 1911
Galerie von Negelein

97

Max Slevogt (1868–1932)
Still Life with Eggs and Citrus Fruits, 1925
Private collection

98

Max Slevogt (1868–1932)
Fruit Still Life, 1911
Staatliche Kunsthalle Karlsruhe

99

Max Slevogt (1868–1932)
Still Life with Apples, Grapes, and Plums, 1914
Private collection

100

Lovis Corinth (1858–1925)
Yellow and Red Asters, 1921
Galerie Paffrath

101

Lovis Corinth (1858–1925)
Flower Still Life (Calla Lilies and Lilacs with Bronze Figure), 1920
Von der Heydt-Museum Wuppertal

102

LESSER URY (1861–1931)
Bouquet of Lilacs, 1922
Staatliche Museen zu Berlin, Nationalgalerie

103

Heinrich Hübner (1869–1945)
Larkspurs, 1913
Staatliche Museen zu Berlin, Nationalgalerie

Theatricality

Big Emotions on Stage and on Canvas

Ortrud Westheider

Theatricality was an important theme in German painting at the beginning of the twentieth century. Ancient and Biblical materials were modernized to express big emotions on canvas. Liebermann, Slevogt, and Corinth employed the spontaneous brushwork of Impressionism to lend performative drama to their pictures. Their painting became the resonance chamber for contemporaneous innovations in theater and modern dance. The battle of the sexes in the stories of Salome and Judith or mythological abduction scenes became more volatile with the emancipation of women—both on stage and on canvas.

In the annual exhibition of the Berlin Secession in 1902, Max Liebermann showed his large-format painting *Samson and Delilah* (cat. 111). Two years earlier, in *Salome II* (fig. 1), Lovis Corinth had already dramatized a woman's fateful art of seduction. Liebermann dispensed with any exotic accoutrements. He presents a man and a woman naked on rumpled sheets. The light of the painting gathers around the woman's slender body. Delilah raises her arm in a triumphant gesture, as if presenting Samson's shorn locks to a theater audience. Liebermann turned the seductive femme fatale of the nineteenth century into a modern woman whose plan is falling into place.[1] In a sober mise-en-scène, the woman is disempowering the man. With her upward movement, she dominates the pictorial space, while the athletic male body lies collapsed on her lap—robbed of its supernatural powers, as the Old Testament text had described it.

In Max Slevogt's painting *The Abduction* (cat. 113), by contrast, the man overpowers the woman. The depiction recalls the mythological scenes of sexualized violence in the work of Peter Paul Rubens—for example, his painting *Rape of the Sabine Women* (ca. 1635–40, National Gallery, London) or *Rape of the Daughters of Leucippus* (ca. 1618, Alte Pinakothek, Munich).[2] But Slevogt's motif cannot by identified with any traditional scene. His male main character is concealing his genitals behind an oversized quiver. His exotic turban seems to have been taken from a different prop room than the woman's indigenous headdress. The scene is identifiably a burlesque in a local palm garden in which the painter's models are role-playing.[3] Slevogt employs persiflage to strip the awful scene of its horrors.[4] The provocation now lies instead in a violation of a previously unchallenged subject of history painting and its romanticizing conception of raping a woman.

Following the model of Édouard Manet (fig. 3), Slevogt established the role portrait in German Impressionism with Francisco d'Andrade in the role of Don Giovanni. Mozart's opera, which the artist had heard with the Portuguese baritone in Munich in 1894, was performed at the Theater des Westens in Berlin in 1902.[5] Slevogt painted d'Andrade's performance from a loge (fig. p. 55). For *The Champagne Aria* (cat. 115), Slevogt decided on a triumphant aria, the opera's musical climax.[6] He had attended a performance in which the temperamental singer increased the aria's already racing staccato. The conductor is said to have tossed aside his baton and left the orchestra to follow the baritone's tempo.[7] This excessive energy is the painting's theme; the Impressionist brushwork underscores the performative effect. Slevogt wanted to derive theatricality from reality as well. His painting thus resonates with theater studies, a field that was just becoming established at the time and gave the performance primacy over the text.[8]

Slevogt returned to this motif a year later, in 1903. The singer and the painter had become friends in the meantime. In the painting *D'Andrade in Black* (cat. 114), the painter rendered the final scene in which Don Giovanni reaches his hand out to the Stone Guest. The bright surroundings of the stage set in "D'Andrade in White" becomes a dark plane that causes the yellow costume to glow. In 1912 Slevogt took up the theme again. The monumental painting *Singer Francisco d'Andrade as Don Giovanni in Mozart's Opera* (cat. 116) was purchased by the Nationalgalerie in Berlin—the museum's first acquisition of a painting by Slevogt.

1
Lovis Corinth,
Salome II, 1900,
Museum der bildenden Künste Leipzig

2
Edgar Degas,
Orchestra Musicians, ca. 1870,
Musée d'Orsay, Paris

The painter's enthusiasm for spectacular performances included modern dance, which around the turn of the century was creating sensations in Loïe Fuller's performances. Slevogt's paintings *Dancer in Gold* (cat. 109) and *Dancer in Silver* (cat. 110) are sketches for a triptych whose central panel, *Dancer in Green*, is lost.[9] Slevogt studied Fuller's stage practices, which included the use of colored light.[10]

Slevogt and Corinth were two of the visual artists whom theater director Max Reinhardt engaged to design sets during his early years in Berlin to achieve his idea of the stage as a space of illusion. Corinth, the painter of *Salome* (fig. 1), worked with sculptor Max Kruse to make the backdrops for Oscar Wilde's eponymous tragedy, which Reinhardt presented at his Kleines Theater in Berlin in 1902.[11] Reinhardt cast Gertrud Eysoldt in the title role, whose intense acting style reflected his programmatic turn from Naturalist to Expressionist theater. In 1903 Corinth painted a role portrait of her (cat. 112). It shows the actor before a bare brick wall and dispenses with the exotic attributes of his earlier Salome and of the stage set. Eysoldt determined the costumes and choreography and, as the dancers Isadora Duncan and Loïe Fuller were also doing at the time, performed barefoot. The dance of the veils by Salome—the personification of the femme fatale for artists of the nineteenth century such as Gustave Moreau—was for Eysoldt an emancipatory act of female self-empowerment in the male-dominated world of the theater—with correspondingly positive backing from women in the audience.[12]

Translated from German by Steven Lindberg

3
Édouard Manet,
Singer Jean-Baptiste Faure as Hamlet, 1877,
Museum Folkwang, Essen

104

Max Liebermann (1847–1935)
Self-Portrait, 1934
Tate, London

105

Max Liebermann (1847–1935)
Self-Portrait in Suit at the Easel, 1922
Galerie Bastian, Berlin

106

Lovis Corinth (1858–1925)
Julius Meier-Graefe, 1912
Musée d'Orsay, Paris

107

Lovis Corinth (1858–1925)
Woman with Wineglass, 1918
Von der Heydt-Museum Wuppertal

108

Lovis Corinth (1858–1925)
Portrait of Mrs. Douglas (Irma Hübner), 1909
Museum der bildenden Künste Leipzig

109

Max Slevogt (1868–1932)
Dancer in Gold, 1895
Landesmuseum Mainz

110

Max Slevogt (1868–1932)
Dancer in Silver, 1895
Landesmuseum Mainz

111

Max Liebermann (1847–1935)
Samson and Delilah, 1902
Städel Museum, Frankfurt am Main

112

Lovis Corinth (1858–1925)
Gertrud Eysoldt as Salome, 1903
Klassik Stiftung Weimar

113

Max Slevogt (1868–1932)
The Abduction, 1905
Niedersächsisches Landesmuseum Hannover

114

Max Slevogt (1868–1932)
D'Andrade in Black, 1903
Hamburger Kunsthalle

115

Max Slevogt (1868–1932)
The Champagne Aria, 1902
Staatsgalerie Stuttgart

116

Max Slevogt (1868–1932)
Singer Francisco d'Andrade as Don Giovanni in Mozart's Opera, 1912
Staatliche Museen zu Berlin, Nationalgalerie

Daniel Zamani

Paradise on the Wannsee

Liebermann's Garden

In 1909 Max Liebermann purchased property on the Wannsee and commissioned designs not only for a villa but also for a spacious garden. From 1915–16 onward, he dedicated himself with great determination to depicting this lavishly planted, self-created paradise. With the immediacy of plein-air painting, the artist emulated the landscapes of the French Impressionists and presented many perspectives on the various areas of its terrain in more than two hundred paintings: the flower garden, the kitchen garden, the gardener's hut, the Wannsee terrace, and the birch forest.

After his father died, Max Liebermann received a considerable inheritance in 1894, making him financially independent. It included the town house at Pariser Platz 7, which had been in the family's possession since 1857; Liebermann and his wife, Martha, had already moved there in 1892. This stately building was located directly next to the Brandenburg Gate and would remain Liebermann's main residence (fig. p. 270) until his death in 1935. In 1909 the painter also purchased a large property in the villa colony Alsen in Wannsee. The house that the artist had built there, designed by architect Paul Otto Baumgarten in the style of Hamburg Neoclassicism, became his summer residence (fig. p. 274). The villa was surrounded by an elaborately designed garden whose geometric beds and clear structure reflected the ideas of the garden reform movement. For the design of his self-created paradise, Liebermann consulted the director of the Hamburger Kunsthalle: art historian Alfred Lichtwark, who had been a friend since the 1890s.

With nearly two hundred documented depictions of it from 1915–16 onward, his Wannsee garden became the principal motif of Liebermann's late Impressionist painting. It had been preceded by numerous views of the bourgeoisie at leisure outdoors, in which he explored the interesting interplay of shadow and light, including views of the zoo in Amsterdam (see cat. 48), in which the artist was already working with brilliant colors and stark tonal contrasts. At the same time, Liebermann was aware of the great importance of gardens and parks in French Impressionism (figs. 1–3). Édouard Manet's large-format work *In the Conservatory* (fig. p. 22) had already entered the collection of the Nationalgalerie in Berlin in 1896. Liebermann consulted his friend Hugo von Tschudi, the museum's director, on acquisitions of French modernism. Three years later, Manet's monumental magnum opus *The Luncheon on the Grass* (fig. p. 23) and his garden painting *The House at Rueil* (fig. 2) were among the six works by the artist on view in an exhibition of the Kunstsalon of cousins Bruno and Paul Cassirer. The painting was also acquired by the Nationalgalerie in 1906, and its tight framing and use of a sunlit, yellowish façade may have inspired Liebermann's later paintings of his gardener's house on the Wannsee (cats. 120, 122, 132).

Due to his financial resources, the painter was able to strategically assemble his own collection of French Impressionism. Among the numerous landscapes that Liebermann acquired were Manet's *Young Girl in the Garden* (1880, private collection) and Claude Monet's *Manet Painting in Monet's Garden in Argenteuil* (1874, lost)—a composition that was also a manifesto for the importance of plein-air painting. This makes it scarcely surprising that Liebermann tried to emulate the style of his French role models, especially in his late garden scenes. Whereas for his early Impressionist paintings he had always done preparatory studies and often worked on their compositions over a considerable span of time in his studio, far from the motif, he did his garden pictures in situ, painting them without previous sketches with the immediacy of the *alla prima* technique. In many works, energetic brushwork and wet-in-wet painting convey an impression of freshness and dynamism. Also typical are the pastose application of paint, which sometimes lends his compositions a striking relief structure, and the use of close framing whose apparent randomness makes the works look like photographic snapshots.

Viewed as a series, Liebermann's garden paintings, which are often sketchlike, focus on the spontaneous reproduction of nature shaped by human hand

1
Claude Monet,
The Artist's Garden at Vétheuil, 1881,
National Gallery of Art, Washington

2
Édouard Manet,
The House at Rueil, 1882,
Alte Nationalgalerie, Berlin

and flooded by sunlight. He knew how to structure a painting with highly differentiated shades of fresh green by adding strong accents in red, blue, pink, orange, and violet. Much like Monet in Giverny, Liebermann wanted to give his own garden a "painterly" look from early on. By choosing plants, he could influence in advance the color scheme of his compositions like a theatrical open-air stage set. At the beginning of the twentieth century, the artist had already grappled intensely with new ideas about garden design and was able to build his knowledge not only in exchange with Alfred Lichtwark, among others, but also thanks to his appointment to Berlin's department of parks in 1904. During a visit to influential garden and gardening author Karl Foerster, Liebermann is said to have studied in detail different varieties of delphinium and emphasized the importance of the right shades of blue for the interplay of colors in the beds—an accent that he achieved in his depictions of the Wannsee terrace by incorporating flanking planters with blue-violet agapanthus flowers (cat. 126).

3
Édouard Manet,
A Garden Nook at Bellevue, 1880,
Kunsthaus Zürich, Emil Bührle Collection

The overwhelming majority of Liebermann's views of gardens are pictorial spaces that are devoid of people and foreground the rich growth of the beds. When figures are included in the composition—whether a female gardener on the edge of the path (cat. 130) or the artist's granddaughter accompanied by her governess (cat. 117)—they are always subordinated to the landscape, and their harmonious embedding in nature underscores the emphatically idyllic quality of his garden paintings. Liebermann began to exhibit his Wannsee works early on, and his splendid flower garden soon played a considerable role in how the public perceived the painter. German journalist Lise Leibholz, who visited the artist in his summer house in 1928, reported that she was impressed by the elaborate, well-manicured grounds that Liebermann had created with Lichtwark's help: "No other house in Wannsee can have such flowerbeds," she wrote with enthusiasm, continuing: "Flowers and still more flowers, cottage-garden flowers, pale red, deep red carnations, roses."[1] For Liebermann, however, his paradise was not just a display of ornamental flowers. For the painter, who was profoundly embittered by the growing antisemitism of nationalist Germans, his summer house by the Wannsee was an existential refuge as well—a modern *hortus conclusus,* in which Liebermann could flee every summer into the "quiet joy of familial idyll."[2]

Translated from German by Steven Lindberg

117

Max Liebermann (1847–1935)
The Artist's Granddaughter with Her Governess in the Wannsee Garden, 1923
Museo Nacional Thyssen-Bornemisza,
Carmen Thyssen Collection, Madrid

118

Max Liebermann (1847–1935)
The Kitchen Garden in Wannsee to the Southeast, 1923
Private collection

119

MAX LIEBERMANN (1847–1935)
The Kitchen Garden in Wannsee to the Northwest, 1923
Private collection

120

Max Liebermann (1847–1935)
Perennials at the Gardener's House to the Northeast, 1926
Private collection, Cologne, courtesy Galerie Paffrath

121

Max Liebermann (1847–1935)
Wannsee Garden—House with Red Perennials, 1926
Galerie Bastian, Berlin

122

Max Liebermann (1847–1935)
Perennials at the Gardener's House to the East, 1923
Private collection

123

Max Liebermann (1847–1935)
Perennials in the Kitchen Garden to the Southwest, 1926
Private collection, courtesy Lempertz, Cologne

124

Max Liebermann (1847–1935)
The Flowerbeds in the Wannsee Garden to the Northwest, 1916
Kunstmuseum Solothurn, Dübi-Müller-Stiftung

125

Max Liebermann (1847–1935)
The Flowerbeds in the Wannsee Garden to the Northwest, 1921
Kunstmuseum Gelsenkirchen

126

Max Liebermann (1847–1935)
The Flowerbeds in the Wannsee Garden to the South, 1921
Private collection

127

Max Liebermann (1847–1935)
Garden Bench Under the Chestnut Tree—Flowering Chestnuts, 1916
Private collection

128

Max Liebermann (1847–1935)
The Birch Path in the Wannsee Garden to the Southwest, 1924
Kunstsammlungen Chemnitz

129

Max Liebermann (1847–1935)
The Kitchen Garden in Wannsee to the Northeast—Perennials, 1916
Private collection

130

Max Liebermann (1847–1935)
The Kitchen Garden in Wannsee to the West, with a Gardener on the Path, ca. 1924
Private collection

131

Max Liebermann (1847–1935)
My House in Wannsee with the Garden, ca. 1926
Private collection

132

Max Liebermann (1847–1935)
Perennials in Front of the Gardener's House to the North, 1928
Private collection

Notes

Essays

The First Avant-Garde:
Impressionism in Germany
Ortrud Westheider
pages 20–29

1 Harry Graf Kessler, in *In memoriam Paul Cassirer: Gedächtnisreden von Max Liebermann [und] Harry Graf Kessler bei der Totenfeier und ein Nachruf von René Schickele,* Weimar 1926, 5–11, here 11. Unless otherwise noted, all translations are by Melissa M. Thorson.

2 See Heinrich Wölfflin, *Kunstgeschichtliche Grundbegriffe: Das Problem der Stilentwicklung in der neueren Kunst,* ed. Hubert Faensen, Dresden 1983, 31–32.

3 In his autobiographical sketch *Mon cœur mis à nu* (1859–65), Charles Baudelaire criticized the concept of the avant-garde for its inherent tendency toward discipline and conformity. See Karlheinz Barck, "Avantgarde," in Barck et al., *Ästhetische Grundbegriffe,* vol. 1, Heidelberg 2010, 555.

4 See Mommsen 1994, 55.

5 See ibid., 39. This difference was already noted by contemporaries: "Also interesting here is the fundamental contrast between artistic developments in France and Germany. In France, it is Paris alone, while in Germany the beneficial development of various art centers both old and new, each of which brings a certain local character, is advantageously apparent." Julius Meier-Graefe, "Die Kunst auf der Weltausstellung," in *Die Weltausstellung in Paris 1900,* ed. Meier-Graefe, Paris 1900, 81–104, here 87; see also Leipzig 2019.

6 Sabine Meister, "Die Vereinigung der XI: Die Künstlergruppe als Keimzelle der organisierten Moderne in Berlin," PhD diss., Universität Freiburg, 2006, urn:nbn:de:bsz:25-opus-27699 (accessed on June 18, 2025).

7 Anja Walter-Ris, "Der moderne Kunsthandel an Spree und Rhein von 1850–1918," ch. 1 in *Die Geschichte der Galerie Nierendorf: Kunstleidenschaft im Dienst der Moderne Berlin/New York 1920–1995,* PhD diss., Freie Universität Berlin, 2003, 24–45, here 25, https://www.google.com/url?sa=t&source=web&rct=j&opi=89978449&url=https://refubium.fu-berlin.de/bitstream/handle/fub188/2107/02_kap1.pdf%3Fsequence%3D3%26isAllowed%3Dy&ved=2ahUKEwjE--WEnomKAxU6gfoHHSRRMnIQFnoECCUQAQ&usg=AOvVaw2nMbYnkG7pqr7koWr3dn8K (accessed on June 18, 2025).

8 Exhibitions with works by artists such as Monet, Morisot, and Renoir were shown in association with world's fairs beginning with the World's Columbian Exposition in Chicago in 1893.

9 Küster 1988, 88–89.

10 Julia Drost, commentary on François Thiébault-Sisson, "L'Art dans les écoles étrangères" [1890], in *Deutsche Kunst: Französische Perspektiven 1870–1945; Quellen und Kommentare zur Kunstkritik,* ed. Friederike Kitchen and Julia Drost, Berlin 2007, 44–48. The original article was published in *La Nouvelle Revue* 62 (1890), 132–54, here 132–33 and 139–41.

11 See ibid., 47–48.

12 See Paul Michael Lützeler, "The St. Louis World's Fair of 1904 as a Site of Cultural Transfer: German and German-American Participation," in *German Culture in Nineteenth-Century America: Reception, Adaptation, Transformation,* ed. Lynne Tatlock et al., Woodbridge 2005, 59–86, here 64, https://doi.org/10.1515/9781571136657-007.

13 At previous world's fairs they had still felt represented, since the buildings created for the World's Columbian Exposition in Chicago in 1893 and the Exposition Universelle in Paris in 1900 referenced German town halls of the sixteenth century and the bourgeois culture of the imperial cities. In 1904, this was replaced by a narrow historical understanding focused exclusively on the Hohenzollern dynasty. See Alfred P. Hagemann, "August Ungers 'Deutsches Haus' auf der Weltausstellung in St. Louis 1904," in *BildGeschichte* 8 (February 3, 2017), https://recs.hypotheses.org/1020 (accessed on June 18, 2025).

14 Bruno Paul, "Die offizielle Berliner Kunst in Saint Louis," front page of *Simplicissimus: Illustrierte Wochenschrift* 8,46 (1904).

15 "As utopian as it may seem today, I nevertheless feel that when the value and the basic requirements of a rich development of art are clearly recognized, a generation of cultural politicians will be created, politicians who will not wish to regulate art by the state—as is the case today in Prussia—but will try to use the power of the state to protect the distinctiveness of art from being crushed and open opportunities that allow talented artists to create in a free manner according to their consciences." Harry Graf Kessler, "Der deutsche Künstlerbund," in *Kunst und Künstler* 2 (1904), 191–96, here 195–96; translated from German by Tas Skorupa.

16 *New York Times,* February 17, 1904.

17 The early French socialists were the first to use the military term in an artistic context; in 1825, Saint-Simonist Olinde Rodriguez wrote, "C'est nous, artistes, qui vous servirons d'avantgarde; la puissance des arts est en effet la plus immédiate et la plus rapide." (We, the artists, will serve as the avant-garde: for amongst all the arms at our disposal, the power of the Arts is the swiftest and most expeditious.) Olinde Rodriguez, "L'Artiste, le savant et l'industriel (1825)," in Claude Henri de Saint-Simon, *Œuvres,* vol. 5, Paris 1960, 204; English translation in *Art in Theory, 1815–1900: An Anthology of Changing Ideas,* ed. Charles Harrison, Paul Wood, and Jason Gaiger, Oxford 1998, 40.

18 Anja Zimmermann, "Avantgarde," in *Metzler Lexikon Kunstwissenschaft,* ed. Ulrich Pfisterer, Stuttgart 2011, https://doi.org/10.1007/978-3-476-00331-7_16.

19 See Théodore Duret, *Critique d'avant-garde,* Paris 1885. The term *avant-garde* is often applied only to anti-bourgeois art since Expressionism. See Corona Hepp, *Avantgarde: Moderne Kunst, Kulturkritik und Reformbewegungen nach der Jahrhundertwende,* Munich 1987. Literary-theoretical studies of the 1980s investigated the disruptive intermediality of the new media of collage and film in the 1920s and described how both artists and elites in the socialist revolution identified with the term. Scholars such as Peter Bürger criticized progressive-theoretical developments in modernism. See Peter Bürger, *Theorie der Avantgarde,* Frankfurt am Main 1974.

20 See Anne Distel, *Impressionism: The First Collectors,* New York 1990, 56–61.

21 See Griselda Pollock on the view that in the 1880s, the term *avant-garde* was not yet in use in France; Griselda Pollock, *Avant-Garde Gambits, 1888–1893: Gender and the Color of Art History,* London 1992, 14.

22 See Duret 1885 (see note 19), 100–01.

23 See ibid., 64.

24 See ibid., 13–14.

25 Letter from Max Liebermann to Théodore Duret (April 15, 1901), in Liebermann 2012, no. 411, 394–95.

26 Letter from Max Liebermann to Théodore Duret (March 15, 1908), in Liebermann 2014, no. 133, 150–51.

27 Théodore Duret, "Claude Monet und der Impressionismus," in *Kunst und Künstler* 2 (1904), 233–45.

28 *Cicerone: Halbmonatsschrift für die Interessen des Kunstforschers und Sammlers* (1909), 441: "Manet occupe aujourd'hui en Allemagne une plus haute place, dans l'opinion générale, que celle qu'il a pu conquérir en France. . . . Ce sont les Allemands qui les premiers ont vu juste et qui, en voyant juste, ont les premiers mis à sa place réelle l'art de Manet."

29 In 1889 the Nationalgalerie had acquired the painting *The Flax Barn at Laren* from 1887, the first by Liebermann to enter a museum collection.

30 "Whether he is using the German loan word here only in a figurative, general sense, or whether he is alluding specifically to the conflict between the German government and the Catholic clergy, and thus implicitly to the tensions between Protestant-influenced Prussia and Catholic-dominated France, remains uncertain. He would have been familiar with the connotation of the word." Drost 2007 (see note 10), 40. On the internationalization of Impressionism, see also Guillaume Apollinaire in *La Peinture moderne* (1913; first published in German in 1908 as "Die moderne Malerei" in Herwarth Walden's *Der Sturm*), who declared Impressionism to be a "manifestation . . . de la culture universellé" supported by artists from all countries.

31 See Harry Graf Kessler, *Impressionisten: die Begründer der modernen Malerei in ihren Hauptwerken: 60 Matt-Tonbilder mit einleitendem Text und einem Catalogue Raisonné,* Munich 1908.

32 See Kern 1989, 126–41. This was also the context for the publication of Meier-Graefe's *Entwicklungsgeschichte der modernen Kunst* in 1904.

33 The art critic, who came from a Jewish merchant family in Hamburg, initially studied art at the Akademie der Bildenden Künste (Academy of Fine Arts) in Munich. See Alexander Bastek, "Der Kunstkritiker Emil Heilbut," master's thesis, Hamburg, 2001; Hendrik Ziegler, "Emil Heilbut: Ein früher Apologet Claude Monets," in *Die Moderne und ihre Sammler: Französische Kunst in deutschem Privatbesitz vom Kaiserreich zur Weimarer Republik,* ed. Andrea Pophanken and Felix Billeter, Berlin 2001, 41–65; and Sabine Schlenker, *Mit dem "Talent der Augen": Der Kunstkritiker Emil Heilbut (1861–1921); Ein Streiter für die moderne Kunst im Deutschen Kaiserreich,* Weimar 2007.

34 Herman Helferich [Emil Heilbut], "Studie über den Naturalismus und Max Liebermann," in *Die Kunst für Alle* 14 (1887), 209–14; 15, 225–29.

35 Ibid., 225: "And if at the beginning of this study we spoke of Zola's nihilists and anarchists, . . . it is not at all unsymbolic, for Liebermann, too—the artistic Liebermann—has something *intransigent* about him; he is the most outstanding of the German Naturalists, unconstrained, unleashed, never slick and entrapped, as all, all of the others seem to quietly, continually, gradually become. He does not grow tame." Italics added by author.

36 Although the artists had adopted the neutral name "Société Anonyme," critics accused them of having an agenda. The plein-air painters around Monet were called the "Intransigents." See Ernest Chesneau, "Au Salon: Avertissement préalable," in *Paris-Journal,* May 9, 1874, and *Le Soir,* May 9, 1874, reprinted in Ruth Berson, *The New Painting: Impressionism 1874–1886; Documentation,* 2 vols., San Francisco 1996, vol. 1, 19.

37 Heilbut 1887 (see note 34), 229.

38 Ibid., 225.

39 Ibid., 228.

40 With regard to the new generation of art critics, Sabine Schlenker writes, "The new critics no longer saw themselves as the lofty judges of art, but as companions of the young artists whose work they wanted to make understandable. They increasingly showed themselves as friends to those artists who were dissatisfied with the exhibition policies and practices of the major Salons and art associations and who, from the 1890s on, formed their own artists' groups or Secessions." Schlenker 2007 (see note 33), 28.

41 Heilbut 1887 (see note 34), 228. Heilbut continued his journalistic advocacy for the art of Max Liebermann: see Herman Helferich [Emil Heilbut], "Studie über den Naturalismus und Max Liebermann II," in *Die Kunst für Alle* 15 (1897), 225–28; and Helferich, *Kunst und Künstler* 1,4 (1902–03), 133–43, where he observes, "In the 1880s, one could write a study about him, 'Naturalism and Max Liebermann,' and if one were young enough, one could still encapsulate him in a school even now; perhaps in a study today one would call the essay 'Liebermann and Impressionism,' and yet he is as little a Naturalist as he is an Impressionist; he is a personality" (142).

42 Heilbut's advocacy for the painter supported Alfred Lichtwark's purchases for the Hamburg Kunsthalle. In 1893 the art critic was among the founding members of the Gesellschaft Hamburgischer Kunstfreunde (Hamburg Society of Friends of Art) and expanded its network of supporters. On behalf of collectors Erdwin and Antonie Almsinck and Eduard Behrends, Heilbut scouted in France for works by painters of the Barbizon School. See Schlenker 2007 (see note 33), 247.

43 "I have taken the liberty of sending you two articles Helferich wrote about me" (letter from Max Liebermann to Wilhelm Bode [April 11, 1888], in Liebermann 2011, 83, no. 51). "That Heilbut speaks so approvingly of me is extremely gratifying to hear. H. is, after all, the finest critic in Germany" (letter from Max Liebermann to Albert Kollmann [after February 20, 1895], in Liebermann 2011, 407–08, no. 349). "Many thanks for your postcard, which Dr. Lichtwark delivered to me at the train station yesterday, where the illustrious of the Hanseatic city—Brinckmann, Lichtwark, Heilbut—had gathered to show the 'infamous' Berliner the Vierlande" (letter from Max Liebermann to Wilhelm Bode [July 17, 1890], in Liebermann 2011, 124–26, no. 88). "With warmest greetings to you, Licht(wark), and—(Heil)but" (letter from Max Liebermann to Thomas Herbst [September 20, 1890], in Liebermann 1911, 138–40, no. 98). "In selecting the printed material to send to you, I paid special attention to who was writing, how he was writing, and what he was writing. Of course, most of it is by Helferich (Heilbut) and Muther, who probably are the most talented of the Germans" (letter from Max Liebermann to Jan Veth [September 28, 1897], in Liebermann 2011, 148–50, no. 147.

44 Heilbut sold Monet's *Road at la Cavée in Pourville* to Durand-Ruel in 1897 as well as the *Boat on the Seine near Jeufosse* in 1900. From 1899 on, *Belle-Île, Sunset* belonged to a private collection in Cologne. *Vineyards in the Snow, Looking Towards the Mill at Orgemont* (1873, Virginia Museum of Fine Arts, Richmond) was acquired by Dresden collector Adolf Rothermundt by 1910 at the latest. See Ziegler 2001 (see note 33, notes 15–17).

45 Emil Heilbut, "Claude Monet," *Freie Bühne für modernes Leben,* March 26, 1890. Heilbut's obituary noted, "Heilbut was one of the few art writers who based himself entirely on the artist's work. He himself had been a painter in Munich and Paris and knew from the studio how to think and appreciate.... His importance, his exemplary character, lies in the fact that he was one of the first in Germany to strive for this unconditional rightness of evaluation, that he wanted to receive the standard of judgment only from the object." See *Kunst und Künstler* 19 (1921), 235–36.

46 See Emil Heilbut, "Zola als Kunstkritiker," in *Die Zukunft* 41 (1902), 65–75.

47 See Liebermann 2013, 119, no. 115. Although the nine-volume edition of Liebermann's letters contains only this one letter to Heilbut, the two are known to have corresponded regularly, since Liebermann mentions Heilbut multiple times in letters to other people. For example: "In fact, I received Heilbut's lines yesterday, in which he communicated to me that Herr Behrens was pleased with my pastel" (letter from Max Liebermann to Alfred Lichtwark [September 4, 1890], in Liebermann 2011, 134–35, no. 95). "About fourteen days ago, Heilbut suddenly came to me, for the first time in fact, in order to select a couple of studies for a gentleman in Hamburg. He took about six of them with him, two of which were acquired by the gentleman in question and one by himself. In that regard, he wrote me enthusiastic letters, in short, he was as if transformed since the time I last saw him in Hamburg" (letter from Max Liebermann to Albert Kollmann [January 23, 1893], in Liebermann 2011, 267–69, no. 214). "About fourteen days ago, Heilbut wrote me from Paris that he had had influenza and thus had not yet returned" (letter from Max Liebermann to Thomas Herbst [October 19, 1894], in Liebermann 2011, 382–84, no. 321). "I am sending you the enclosed letter from Heilbut and herewith convey to you that I answered him, saying that I received the acceptance of his offer from the owner of the picture—without mentioning your name" (letter from Max Liebermann to Albert Kollmann [March 29, 1895], in Liebermann 2011, 420, no. 360).

48 See Anna Maria Pfäfflin, "'Nichts ist Nebensache in einem Bilde": Die Zeichnungen von Caspar David Friedrich im Berliner Kupferstichkabinett," in *Caspar David Friedrich: Unendliche Landschaften,* exh. cat., Alte Nationalgalerie, Berlin 2024, 93–105, here 99.

49 *Van Gogh: Fields; The Field with Poppies and the Artists' Dispute,* exh. cat., Kunsthalle Bremen 2002.

Max Liebermann:
The Reception of French Impressionism in the German Kaiserreich
Barbara Schaefer
pages 30–39

1 Art critic Louis Leroy was the first to refer to the exhibiting artists as "Impressionists" in 1874 (Louis Leroy, "L'Exposition des impressionnistes," in *Le Charivari,* April 25, 1874, 79–80). Four days later, the term *Impressionism* was used for the first time by Jules-Antoine Castagnary (*Le Siècle,* April 29, 1874, 3).

2 On the history of Fritz Gurlitt's art gallery, see Birgit Gropp, "Studien zur Kunsthandlung Fritz Gurlitt in Berlin 1880–1943," PhD diss., Freie Universität Berlin, 2000.

3 Anonymous, "Eine Sammlung von Gemälden der sogenannten 'Impressionisten,'" in *Über Land und Meer: Allgemeine Illustrirte Zeitung* 51,6 (October 1883–84), 115. Unless otherwise noted, all translations are by Melissa M. Thorson.

4 Max Liebermann, "Meine Erinnerungen an die Familie Bernstein," in Liebermann 1978, 96–101, here 97.

5 Max Liebermann recalled that painter Adolph Menzel, a professor at the academy in Berlin, asked the lady of the house, "Did you really spend money on this rubbish?" Noticing Felicie Bernstein's perplexity, Menzel added, "I'm very sorry to have expressed myself so impolitely about your collection, but it's my honest opinion. Your pictures are hideous"; quoted in ibid., 98. See also Martin Faass, "'Haben Sie wirklich Geld für den Dreck gegeben?'—Wie der Impressionism nach Berlin kam," in Berlin 2013, 162–71.

6 Not every aspect of this multifaceted development can be addressed here; for example, the problem of terminology—from Naturalism/Realism to *Hellmalerei* and *plein air* to the concept of Impressionism itself—will not be further explored in the context of this study. On Max Liebermann's Impressionism, see Stefan Pucks, "Max Liebermann—Vom 'Apostel der Häßlichkeit' zum 'Manet der Deutschen,'" in Vienna 1997, 35–42.

7 The annexation of Alsace and parts of Lorraine were deeply humiliating for the defeated nation of France. On the German side, the primary result of the war was the founding of the Reich in January 1871, long desired by many Germans.

8 In contrast to France, where the rise of middle-class society had already begun to undermine the academic hierarchy of painting genres in the early nineteenth century, it was not until after 1871 that a bourgeoisie oriented to the private sphere emerged in Germany. This development was accompanied on the art market by the decline of interest in history paintings with civic themes—the result of a gradually occurring social change in the German Empire.

9 Quoted in Wolfgang Born, "Max Liebermann," in *Reclams Universum* 43,16 (1927), 446.

10 Max Liebermann, "Degas," in *PAN* 4,2 (November 1896), 164.

11 Kern 1989, 18.

12 See the detailed discussion in Birgit Jooss, "München als Ursprungsort des deutschen Impressionismus," in Bielefeld 2009, 51–60.

13 Ibid., 53.

14 See Eberhard Ruhmer, "Leibl als Vorbild," in Munich 1994, 155–75.

15 Kern 1989, 55.

16 *Aufstieg und Fall der Moderne: Weimar—ein deutsches Beispiel 1890–1990,* exh. cat., Kunstsammlungen zu Weimar 1999.

17 Later, Liebermann would also serve as president of the Akademie der Künste in Berlin (1920–32) and as its honorary president from 1932 on, before resigning from the academy on May 7, 1933, following the seizure of power by the Nazi regime.

18 The artistic taste of Wilhelm II and political and social conditions in the German Empire were subjected to increasing criticism in art and literature. The conflict between modernity and conservatism is first manifested in works from the 1890s such as Gerhart Hauptmann's drama *The Weavers* (1892) and Käthe Kollwitz's cycle of prints *A Weavers' Revolt* (1893–97).

19 See also Françoise Forster-Hahn, "Max Liebermann, the Outsider as Impresario of Modernism in the Empire," in Los Angeles 2005, 181–98.

20 For an in-depth discussion of the 1903 exhibition of the Vienna Secession, see Lukas Gloor, *Von Böcklin zu Cézanne: Die Rezeption des französischen Impressionismus in der deutschen Schweiz,* Bern 1986, 76–78.

21 Although it would go beyond the scope of this essay to discuss individual thematic orientations, reasons for particular emphases, or the specific effects on reception history, some of the most important private collections of modern art in the German Empire should be mentioned here: in Berlin, the collection of Eduard Arnhold, the aforementioned Bernstein collection, the collection of Bernhard Koehler, and that of Julius Stern; in Hamburg, the collections of Emil Heilbut and Henry P. Newman; those of Max Linde in Lübeck, Meta Schütte in Bremen, Alfred Flechtheim in Düsseldorf, Karl Ernst Osthaus in Hagen, Martha and Hugo Nathan in Frankfurt am Main, and Oskar Schmitz in Dresden; and the collections of Alfred Wolff, Count Harry Kessler, and Alfred Walter Heymel.

22 Annegret Janda, "Max Liebermanns Kunstsammlung in seinen Briefen: Versuch einer Chronologie," in Vienna 1997, 225–53; see Hedinger et al. 2013.

23 Quoted in Gloor 1986 (see note 20), 84. Other German museum directors also persisted in their efforts to acquire nineteenth-century French art: examples include Alfred Lichtwark at the Hamburger Kunsthalle, Gustav Pauli at the Kunsthalle Bremen, Georg Swarzenski at the Städelsches Kunstinstitut in Frankfurt am Main, Fritz Wichert at the Kunsthalle in Mannheim, Alfred Hagelstange at the Wallraf-Richartz-Museum in Cologne, and Karl Ernst Osthaus at the Museum Folkwang in Hagen.

24 See Berlin 2001.

25 Wilhelm II, “Die wahre Kunst (18.12.1901),” in Wilhelm II, *Reden des Kaisers: Ansprachen, Predigten und Trinksprüche Wilhelms II,* ed. Ernst Johann, Munich 1966, 99–103. English translation in “Wilhelm II, ‘True Art’ (1901),” in *Wilhelmine Germany and The First World War (1890–1918),* German History in Documents and Images, https://ghdi.ghi-dc.org/docpage.cfm?docpage_id=1184 (accessed on March 31, 2025).

26 For a comprehensive discussion of the person and influence of Hugo von Tschudi, see Berlin 1996.

27 Friedrich Pecht, “Über den heutigen französischen Impressionismus,” in *Die Kunst für Alle* 2,22 (1887), 337–39, here 339: “[Die] Adoptierung solcher französischen Moden ... [die] den Deutschen mehr geschadet als genützt [hat].”

28 *Ein Protest deutscher Künstler: Mit Einleitung von Carl Vinnen,* Jena 1911. A riposte followed in *Im Kampf um die Kunst: Die Antwort auf den “Protest deutscher Künstler”; Mit Beiträgen deutscher Künstler, Galerieleiter, Sammler und Schriftsteller,* Munich 1911.

29 Julius Meier-Graefe, *Entwicklungsgeschichte der modernen Kunst: Vergleichende Betrachtung der bildenden Künste, als Beitrag zu einer neuen Aesthetik,* 3 vols., Stuttgart 1904. English translation: *The Development of Modern Art: Being a Contribution to a New System of Aesthetics,* trans. Florence Simmonds and George W. Chrystal, 2 vols., New York 1908.

30 Ibid., 137.

31 Prior to the publication of Meier-Graefe’s text, the pioneering study in Germany was Richard Muther’s *Geschichte der Malerei im XIX. Jahrhundert,* 3 vols., Munich 1893–94.

32 For further discussion, see Julius H. Schoeps, “‘Ick kann jar nich so viel fressen, wie ick kotzen möchte’: Max Liebermann, die Nazis und das Scheitern der deutsch-jüdischen Symbiose,” in Vienna 1997, 43–49.

33 Liebermann 2011–21, vol. 2, 128–29, here 129, no. 131 (July 10, 1897): “Aber es giebt [*sic*] nur ein Land der Welt für die Malerei, c’est la Hollande.”

34 Quoted in Kern 1989, 81.

Everyday Narratives:
Genre Painting in German Impressionism
Alexander Bastek
pages 40–49

1 Louis Leroy, “L’Exposition des impressionnistes,” in *Le Charivari,* April 25, 1874, 79–80; see John Rewald, *The History of Impressionism,* New York 1946, 4th ed. 1973, 318.

2 Ibid., 318–25.

3 Emil Heilbut published his essay under the telling pseudonym Herman Helferich. Herman Helferich, “Studie über den Naturalismus und Max Liebermann,” in *Die Kunst für Alle* 2,14 (1887), 209–14, here 211; continued in 2,15 (1887), 225–29.

4 Gotthold Ephraim Lessing, *Laokoon oder Über die Grenzen der Malerei,* Berlin 1766.

5 Heilbut 1887 (see note 3), 212: “Lachenden oder weinenden Schauspiele.”

6 Liebermann 1978, 28.

7 Bertuleit 1994, 40.

8 Ibid.

9 Friedrich Pecht, “Die Münchener Ausstellungen von 1888: III. Das Sittenbild,” in *Die Kunst für Alle* 3,20 (1888), 307–14, here 311.

10 Bertuleit 1994 (see note 7), 42.

11 Markus Bertsch, “Max Liebermann, Die Netzflickerinnen, 1887/89,” https://online-sammlung.hamburger-kunsthalle.de/de/objekt/HK-1580/die-netzflickerinnen?term=netzflickerinnen&context=default&position=0 (accessed on April 16, 2025).

12 See Ortrud Westheider’s essay in this catalog, 20–29.

13 Letter from Max Liebermann to Gotthardt Kuehl (June 29, 1889), in Liebermann 2011, 113–14, here 114, no. 75.

14 On a personal level and in their attitudes toward each other’s work, however, there were also significant differences. See Heike Biedermann, “Die Gemälde von Max Liebermann in der Dresdner Galerie,” in Dresden 2008, 18–35; and Warzecha 2022.

15 Kuehl signed the painting “G. Kuehl. 84. Paris.”

16 The postcard is illustrated at https://sammlung.museum-behnhaus-draegerhaus.de/werk/luebecker-waisenhaus-43 (accessed on June 27, 2025).

17 Emil Heilbut, “Neuere Arbeiten von Max Liebermann,” in *Kunst und Künstler* 1 (1902–03), 133–43, here 139.

18 On Brütt’s work, see Alexander Bastek, *Ferdinand Brütt und das städtisch bürgerliche Genre um 1900,* Weimar 2007; *Ferdinand Brütt 1849–1936: Erzählung und Impression,* exh. cat., Museum Giersch, Frankfurt am Main 2007.

19 Quoted in Christiane Eisenberg, *“English Sports” und Deutsche Bürger: Eine Gesellschaftsgeschichte 1800–1939,* Paderborn 1999, 199: “[D]aß in gewisser Beziehung Tennisplätze ausgiebiger selbst als Ballsäle seien.... eine rationelle Ausdehnung des Heirathsmarkets.”

20 Emil Heilbut, “Die Sammlung Linde in Lübeck,” *Kunst und Künstler* 2 (1904), 6–20, 303–25.

21 Alexander Bastek, “Heinrich Eduard Linde-Walther: Die Hartengrube in Lübeck,” in *Hundert Meisterwerke: Die Sammlung des Museums Behnhaus Drägerhaus Lübeck,* ed. Bastek, Petersberg 2017, 161.

22 Wolfgang Kemp, *Der Anteil des Betrachters: Rezeptionsästhetische Studien zur Malerei des 19. Jahrhunderts,* Munich 1983, 21.

From Wild Garden to Stage:
The Impressionism of Max Slevogt in Berlin and Neukastel
Karoline Feulner
pages 50–57

1 For extensive biographical information on Slevogt, see Edenkoben 2009, 10–39, here 12, 15.

2 Imiela 1968, 52–54, 121.

3 See the detailed discussion in Nina Nedelykov and Pedro Moreira, “Eine kurze Baugeschichte der Liebermann-Villa,” in Berlin 2010a, 31–34.

4 See Jenns Eric Howoldt, “Der Nutzgarten: ‘Hundert Bilder könnte man hier malen ...,’” in ibid., 77–78; and Petra Wandrey, “Die Blumenterrasse,” in ibid., 99–100.

5 The Slevogthof is a large manor consisting of an inner and front courtyard, a terraced garden, and a tower. It also included various cultivated plots, lawns, and a vineyard. Slevogt acquired the manor in 1914 from the bankruptcy estate of his wife’s parents.

6 See, for example, *Red Leaves with Dog,* 1897, GDKE, Landesmuseum Mainz; *Arbor with Vines at Neukastel,* 1917, Wallraf-Richartz-Museum & Fondation Courboud, Cologne; *Mrs. Slevogt at the Stone Table,* 1921, private collection.

7 See the detailed discussion in Imiela 1968, 230–37, 270–72.

8 For Neukastel and the frescoes in general, see Bernhard Geil, "'sein eigenstes Gesicht . . .': Slevogt gestaltet Neukastel," in Hannover 2018, 124–31.

9 Karl Scheffler, *Die fetten und die mageren Jahre: Ein Arbeits- und Lebensbericht* [1948], Wädenswil 2011, 115: "[S]toßweise, intuitiv und improvisatorisch: er arbeitete ungemein schnell und konzentriert. Ein Bildnis, ein Stilleben wurde oft in wenigen Stunden fertig. Als Zeichner war er Nachtarbeiter."

10 In a letter from August 20, 1926, for example, Bruno Cassirer asks Max Slevogt for "new plans," since he will soon have published all that he has on hand (Landesbibliothekszentrum Rheinland-Pfalz (LBZ) / Pfälzische Landesbibliothek, Speyer, Nachlass Slevogt N 100). Slevogt's terse answer from September 12, 1926, reads: "I'm feeling well again, but only have passion for painting"; Saarlandmuseum, Saarbrücken. Cassirer responds again on September 14, 1926, with a certain degree of humor: "I won't take your graphic refusal so tragically, since as we all know, you always do something different than you had planned"; LBZ / Pfälzische Landesbibliothek, Speyer, Nachlass Slevogt N 100. A research cooperative (Dr. Karoline Feulner, GDKE, Landesmuseum Mainz; Dr. Armin Schlechter, LBZ / Pfälzische Landesbibliothek, Speyer; and Dr. Eva Wolf, Saarlandmuseum, Saarbrücken) is preparing a special exhibition entitled *Auf zu neuen Werken!—Max Slevogt und sein Verleger Bruno Cassirer* for 2025–26. In addition to the exhibition catalog, an annotated edition of the correspondence of Bruno Cassirer and Max Slevogt will be published.

11 Bruno Cassirer, *Max Slevogt: Ein Verzeichnis der von ihm illustrierten Bücher, Mappenwerke und Graphiken,* Berlin 1924, 3.

12 Karoline Feulner, "'Indianer' in den Dünen von Noordwijk: Slevogt's Lederstrumpf-Illustrationen," in Mainz 2018, 150n3. The same is true of *Rübezahl;* see Scheffler 2011 (see note 9), 116.

13 Max Liebermann stated, "In my lifestyle I am the most perfect bourgeois: I eat, drink, sleep, go for walks, and work with the regularity of a church clock." Quoted in Scheer 2017, 246–47.

14 It hung in the exhibition *Schule von Fontainebleau, Französische Impressionisten, Anders Zorn, J. Nussbaum, A. Gaul, Fr. Flaum,* Kunstsalon Bruno & Paul Cassirer, February 24–March 31, 1900; see Bernhard Echte and Walter Feilchenfeldt, *Kunstsalon Cassirer,* vol. 1: *Kunstsalon Bruno & Paul Cassirer: Die Ausstellungen 1898–1901: "Das Beste aus aller Welt zeigen,"* Wädenswil 2011, 253–70.

15 Édouard Manet, *The House at Rueil,* 1882, Alte Nationalgalerie, Berlin Emil Waldmann, *Max Slevogt,* Berlin 1923, 80; Imiela 1968, 121; for a general discussion, see Saarbrücken 2018.

16 "Verzeichnis von Bildern, Aquarellen, Zeichnungen und Kunstgegenständen in eigenem Besitz, nach eigenhändigen Aufzeichnungen von M. Slevogt, transkribiert durch den Sammler F. J. Kohl-Weigand," Saarlandmuseum, Saarbrücken. A bound copy is also in the Landesmuseum Mainz. Édouard Manet, *La Rue Mosnier aux drapeaux,* 1878, private collection. See also Kathrin Elvers-Švamberk, "Slevogt und Frankreich," in Saarbücken 2018, 19–20.

17 Julius Norden, "Aus dem Berliner Kunstleben," in *Magdeburgische Zeitung,* March 9, 1902, quoted in Bernhard Echte and Walter Feilchenfeldt, *Kunstsalon Cassirer,* vol. 2: *Kunstsalon Paul Cassirer: Die Ausstellungen 1901–1905; "Man steht da und staunt,"* Wädenswil 2011, 119.

18 Edenkoben 2009 (see note 1), 12.

19 *Édouard Manet, H. G. E. Degas, P. Puvis de Chavannes, Max Slevogt,* Kunstsalon Bruno & Paul Cassirer, October 15–December 1, 1899; see Echte/Feilchenfeldt 2011 (see note 14), 177–214.

20 Letter from Paul Cassirer to Max Slevogt (September 24, 1899), LBZ / Pfälzische Landesbibliothek, Speyer, Nachlass Max Slevogt N 100. See also Mainz 2018, cats. 2.1, 2.2.

21 Imiela 1968, 362n33.

22 Letter from Max Slevogt to Carl Steinbart (October 23, 1910), GDKE, Landesmuseum Mainz.

23 The first letter from Bruno Cassirer is from July 1, 1899, and a postcard from Paul Cassirer is dated July 29, 1899, both LBZ / Pfälzische Landesbibliothek, Speyer, Nachlass Slevogt N 100.

24 Letter from Bruno Cassirer to Max Slevogt (November 15, 1899), LBZ / Pfälzische Landesbibliothek, Speyer, Nachlass Slevogt N 100.

25 Guthmann 1920, 50.

26 In this context he also met Josef Grünberg, with whom he made experimental prints under the name SPOG together with Emil Orlik and Bernhard Pankok; see *Hexenküche: Max Slevogts druckgrafische Experimente,* exh. cat., Landesmuseum Mainz, 2021. Regarding his network, see Wedekind 2021.

27 Sigrun Paas, "Slevogt und der Tanz," in Edenkoben 2007, 9–21, here 9. On dance and theater as a theme in general, see also Schweinfurt 2022.

28 For a detailed discussion, see Hans-Jürgen Imiela, "Max Slevogt und Francisco d'Andrade," in Edenkoben 1991, 7–44.

29 See Ernest W. Uthemann, "Slevogt und Manet," in Saarbrücken 1992, 109–15.

30 Hans Rosenhagen, "Die fünfte Ausstellung der Berliner Secession," in *Die Kunst für Alle* 2,19 (1902), 433–46, here 436.

31 Karl Scheffler, *Max Slevogt,* Berlin 1940, 7.

32 The final version of the title page shows the motif in altered form: here, the bundle of asparagus is presented by Fama. The copies belonging to Slevogt and his wife are preserved in the artist's estate. Seven lithographs by artists including Emil Orlik, Max Liebermann, and Hans Purrmann were bound together with the title page.

33 On Liebermann's art collection, see Hedinger et al. 2013.

34 Michael Fuhr, "'Slevogts Bilder hängen neben solchen von Manet, Degas und Puvis de Chavannes': Einiges zu Paul Cassirer, Max Slevogt und den Wandmalereien von Neu-Cladow," in *Ein Fest der Künste: Paul Cassirer; Der Kunsthändler als Verleger,* exh. cat., Max Liebermann Haus, Berlin 2006, 297–309, here 298.

35 Anonymous, "Ein Aufsatz Liebermanns," in *Kunst und Künstler* 2 (1903–04), 296–97, here 296.

36 See, for example, *Pineapple,* 1902, Saarlandmuseum, Saarbrücken; *Platter of Meat,* 1930, Landesmuseum Oldenburg; and *Still Life with Watermelon,* ca. 1931, Städel Museum, Frankfurt am Main.

37 Max Slevogt, "Der sogenannte Impressionismus," in Berlin 1928, 6.

Max Liebermann:
Painter and Collector of Impressionism
Lucy Wasensteiner
pages 58–67

1 Max Liebermann, "Claude Monet," *Kunst und Künstler* 25,5 (1927), 163–70, here 163.
2 See Cologne 2024.
3 Unless otherwise noted, biographical information in this text is taken from Eberle 1995–96 and Liebermann 2011–21.
4 Anna Ahrens, "Ein 'Präludium über Malerei': Frühe Begegnungen Max Liebermanns mit französischer Malkunst in Berlin und Weimar," in Berlin 2013, 10–21, here 16–17. See also *Catalogue des tableaux modernes composant l'importante collection de M. le chevalier Adolphe Liebermann de Wahlendorf*, auction catalog Hôtel Drouot, Paris, May 8–9, 1876.
5 See Deshmukh 2015, 23–70.
6 *Verlorene Schätze: Die Kunstsammlung von Max Liebermann*, exh. cat., Liebermann-Villa am Wannsee, Berlin 2013, no. 59.
7 See Barbara Schaefer's essay in this catalog, 30–39.
8 See Anna-Dorothea Ludewig, "'Haben Sie wirklich Geld für den Dreck gegeben?': Die Sammlung Carl und Felicie Bernstein," in Ludewig 2012, 90–103.
9 Berlin 2013 (see note 6), no. 121.
10 Ibid., no. 42. Liebermann had met Degas in 1896 during his trip to Paris with Tschudi; see the letter from Max Liebermann to Alfred Lichtwark (June 5, 1911), in Eberle 1995–96, 86–90.
11 See Berlin 2013 (see note 6), nos. 110, 113, and 118. In 1898 Liebermann owned seven Manets; see the letter from Max Liebermann to Max Linde (September 26, 1898), in Eberle 1995–96, 234–36.
12 Berlin 2013 (see note 6), no. 179.
13 Letter from Max Liebermann to an editor (before April 24, 1909), in Eberle 1995–96, 285–87, here 287.
14 Berlin 2013 (see note 6), no. 178.
15 Ibid., no. 177.
16 Letter from Max Liebermann to Alfred Lichtwark (December 16, 1906), in Eberle 1995–96, 491–92.
17 Liebermann 1927 (see note 1), 168.
18 Berlin 2013 (see note 6), nos. 43 and 41.
19 Ibid., no. 44; see also no. 45.
20 Individual printed works are documented; see, for example, Achenbach 1974, no. 100.
21 Letter from Max Liebermann to Wilhelm Bode (January 1902), in Eberle 1995–96, 17–18, here 18.
22 Berlin 2013 (see note 6), no. 201.
23 Ibid., no. 11.
24 Letter from Max Liebermann to Gustav Pauli (January 27, 1909), in Eberle 1995–96, 251–52.
25 Berlin 2013 (see note 6), nos. 109, 107, 105, and 111.
26 See Michael Diers, "Liebermann und Manet," in Berlin 2013 (see note 6), 77–88.
27 Max Liebermann, "Zwei Original-Holzschnitte von Manet," in *Kunst und Künstler* 3,4 (1905), 140–46; Liebermann, "Ein Beitrag zur Arbeitsweise Manets," *Kunst und Künstler* 8,10 (1910), 483–88.
28 Liebermann 1905 (see note 27), 144.
29 Ibid.
30 Ibid.
31 Berlin 2013 (see note 6), no. 106. See also Diers 2013 (see note 26), 80–81.
32 Letter from Max Liebermann to Julias Elias (April 9, 1903), in Eberle 1995–96, 111–12.
33 Berlin 2013 (see note 6), no. 180.
34 See, for example, *Zeitenwende: Von der Berliner Secession zur Novembergruppe*, exh. cat., Bröhan-Museum, Berlin 2015.
35 See Berlin 2010a.
36 See Erich Hancke, "Der Meister im Atelier," in *Vossische Zeitung*, July 19, 1927, 166.
37 Martin Faass, "Liebermann und Lichtwark: Eine Kunst- und Gartenfreundschaft," in *Neue Gärten! Gartenkunst zwischen Jugendstil und Moderne*, exh. cat., Museum für Gartenkunst, Düsseldorf 2017, 154–67.
38 Berlin 2013 (see note 6), no. 108.
39 Annegret Janda, "Max Liebermann's Kunstsammlung: Eine Chronologie," in Berlin 2013 (see note 6), 11–30, here 19.
40 See *Meeting Liebermann: Fotoporträts aus der Sammlung Ullstein*, exh. cat., Liebermann-Villa am Wannsee, Berlin 2023.
41 See Alfred Lichtwark, "Der Sammler," in *Kunst und Künstler* 10,5 (1912), 229–42, and 10,6, 281–91, with reproductions of eleven works from the Liebermann collection.
42 Marie-Amélie zu Salm-Salm, "Max Liebermann und die französischen Impressionisten: Zwischen Distanz und Nähe," in Berlin 2013, 126–37.
43 Diers 2013 (see note 26), 83.
44 Max Liebermann, *Die Phantasie in der Malerei* [1916], with an afterword by Erich Hancke, Leipzig 1948, 44. Other late purchases of French works include sketches by Manet acquired in 1921 and 1929 (Berlin 2013 [see note 6], nos. 122–23) and an unidentified drawing by Degas acquired in 1932 (no. 48).
45 The post-1933 history of the Liebermann family as recounted here is taken from Schmalhausen 1994.
46 Overview of the collection of Max and Martha Liebermann in the Lost Art database of the Deutsches Zentrum Kulturgutverluste, https://www.lostart.de/de/verlust/person/liebermann-martha-and-max/541894 (accessed on November 25, 2024).
47 Monika Tatzkow and Georg Graf zu Castell-Castell, "Verlorene Schätze? Die Sammlung Liebermann ab 1933," in Berlin 2013 (see note 6), 91–106.
48 Ibid., nos. 105, 109, 111, 112, 113, 121 (works by Manet); 11, 12 (works by Cézanne); 41, 43, 44 (works by Degas); 201 (Renoir); and 178 (Monet). The fourteenth work was an oil painting by Honoré Daumier; ibid., no. 23.
49 See, for example, ibid., nos. 106, 107, 114, 118, 123, and 177.

Catalog of Exhibited Works

Impressionism in Germany:
First Steps
Valentina Plotnikova
pages 68–71

1 Max Liebermann, *Josef Israëls* [1916], 5th ed., Berlin 1918, 30. Unless otherwise noted, all translations are by Steven Lindberg.

2 Eugen Gradmann, "Die Landschaftsmaler," in *Die Stuttgarter Kunst der Gegenwart*, Stuttgart 1913, 103–30, here 111.

3 Hamburg 1997, 114.

4 On this, see the essay by Alexander Bastek in the present volume, 40–49.

5 See the chapter "Paradise on the Wannsee: Liebermann's Garden" in this catalog, 224–27.

6 "I had, however, recommended Uhde Zandvoort, which I had visited in 1875, and he painted the studies for the hurdy-gurdy man there (which is still in my possession)." Letter from Max Liebermann to Gustav Pauli (January 13, 1912), in Liebermann 2015, 181–82, no. 149, here 181.

7 See Richard Hamann and Jost Hermand, *Deutsche Kunst und Kultur von der Gründerzeit bis zum Expressionismus*, vol. 2: *Naturalismus*, Berlin 1959, 160.

8 See the chapter "Freshness and Dynamism: Out in the Open Air" in this catalog, 94–97.

9 See Holly Todd, "Liebermann and the Dutch Landscape: Art and Milieu, Past and Present," in Deshmukh 2011, 35–48, here 36.

10 See Stefan Pucks, "'Hier wohnte und wirkte Max Liebermann': Die Stadtwohnung des Künstlers am Pariser Platz und sein Landhaus am Wannsee," in *Eine Liebe zu Berlin: Künstlersalon und Gartenatelier von Max Liebermann*, ed. Christoph Hölz and Gabriele Kolber, Munich 1995, 12–45, here 16.

11 *Road at La Cavée in Pourville* (1882, private collection), *Boat on the Seine at Jeufosse* (1884, private collection), and *Belle-Île: Sunset* (1886, private collection). See Hendrik Ziegler, "Emil Heilbut: Ein früher Apologet Claude Monets," in *Die Moderne und ihre Sammler: Französische Kunst in deutschem Privatbesitz vom Kaiserreich zur Weimarer Republik*, ed. Andrea Pophanken and Felix Billeter, Berlin 2001, 41–65, here 43.

12 "Fragmentarischer Entwurf von Christian Rohlfs zu einem Lebenslauf (Nachlass K. E. Osthaus)," in Munich 1996a, 269.

13 Meier-Graefe 1904, vol. 2, 533.

14 On the diversity of German Impressionism, see Hamburg 2021, 18–24.

Freshness and Dynamism:
Out in the Open Air
Valentina Plotnikova
pages 94–97

1 Max Liebermann and Philipp Franck had summer homes in Wannsee; Max Slevogt purchased a manor house near Leinsweiler in the Palatinate; Christian Landenberger spent a great deal of time at Lake Constance and the Ammersee, as Fritz von Uhde did at the Starnberger See.

2 See Hamburg 2021, 54.

3 Ernst Braun, "Die Beisetzung Max Liebermanns am 11. Februar 1935: Umstände, Personen, Überlieferungen, Pressereaktionen," in *Jahrbuch der Staatlichen Kunstsammlungen Dresden: Beiträge, Berichte 1985*, vol. 17, Dresden 1987, 167–86, here 170.

4 See Gudrun M. König, *Eine Kulturgeschichte des Spazierganges: Spuren einer bürgerlichen Praktik, 1780–1850*, Vienna 1996, 17–18.

5 See Innsbruck 2003, 95.

6 On Peter Joseph Lenné's conversion of the Tiergarten into a landscape park from 1832 to 1866 see, for example, Folkwin Wendland, *Der Große Tiergarten in Berlin: Seine Geschichte und Entwicklung in fünf Jahrhunderten*, Berlin 1993, 98–191.

7 On the collection's works and history, see *Alfred Lichtwarks "Sammlung von Bildern aus Hamburg,"* exh. cat., Hamburger Kunsthalle, 2002. Unless otherwise noted, all translations are by Steven Lindberg.

8 In 1908–09, the Potsdamer Yacht Club built a new clubhouse; one year later, the Verein Seglerhaus am Wannsee followed with a large new building. See Bremen 2016, 125.

9 Rüdiger Hachtmann, *Tourismus und Tourismusgeschichte*, Potsdam 2010, 67, https://zeitgeschichte-digital.de/doks/frontdoor/deliver/index/docId/312/file/docupedia_hachtmann_tourismusgeschichte_v1_de_2010.pdf (accessed on May 15, 2025).

10 *Die Dame zu Pferde: Briefe eines alten Reitlehrers über den Reitunterricht der Damen*, ed. Helene von Rheiffen, Berlin 1907, 324.

An Eye on Modernity:
Cityscapes
Valentina Plotnikova
pages 122–25

1. In his essay "Le Peintre de la vie moderne," in the newspaper *Le Figaro* in 1863, Charles Baudelaire described the figure of the flaneur: "Pour le parfait flâneur, pour l'observateur passionné, c'est une immense jouissance que d'élire domicile dans le nombre, dans l'ondoyant, dans le mouvant, dans le fugitif et l'infini." (For the perfect flaneur, for the passionate spectator, it is an immense joy to set up house in the heart of the multitude, amid the ebb and flow of movement, in the midst of the fugitive and the infinite). See Charles Baudelaire, "L'Art romantique," in *Œuvres complètes de Charles Baudelaire,* ed. Charles Asselineau, vol. 3, Paris 1885, 65; English translation in *The Painter of Modern Life and Other Essays,* trans. Jonathan Mayne, London 1964, 9.
2. See Hans Schliepmann, "Bier- und Kaffeehäuser," in *Berlin und seine Bauten,* ed. Architekten-Verein zu Berlin und der Vereinigung Berliner Architekten, vol. 3, Berlin 1896, 1–17, here 15.
3. See Lovis Corinth, "Berlin nach dem Krieg," in Englert 1995, 145–49, here 149. This article on Berlin after World War I was first published in the newspaper *Berliner Tageblatt* in 1920. Unless otherwise noted, all translations are by Steven Lindberg.
4. "Now the giant city sucks the country dry, insatiably and incessantly demanding and devouring fresh streams of men, till it wearies and dies in the midst of an almost uninhabited waste of country." See Oswald Spengler, *The Decline of the West: Form and Actuality,* trans. Charles Francis Atkinson, New York 1939, 102.
5. "La rue assourdissante autour de moi hurlait. / Longue, mince, en grand deuil, douleur majestueuse, / Une femme passa, d'une main fastueuse / Soulevant, balançant le feston et l'ourlet." (The deafening road around me roared. / Tall, slim, in deep mourning, making majestic grief, / A woman passed, lifting and swinging / With a pompous gesture the ornamental hem of her garment, // Swift and noble, with statuesque limb.) See Charles Baudelaire, "À une passante (Einer Dame)," in Walter Benjamin, *Tableaux parisiens,* ed. Antonia Birnbaum and Michel Métayer, Berlin 2017, 56–57; English translation in *Selected Poems of Charles Baudelaire,* trans. Geoffrey Wagner, New York 1974.
6. See, for example, Wilhelm Erb, *Über die wachsende Nervosität unserer Zeit,* Heidelberg 1893; Richard von Krafft-Ebing, *Nervosität und Neurosthenische Zustände,* Vienna 1895; and Albert Moll, *Einfluß des großstädtischen Lebens auf das Nervensystem,* Berlin 1902.

Intimate Worlds:
Houses and Gardens
Daniel Zamani
pages 150–53

1. Walter Benjamin, *The Arcades Project,* trans. Howard Eiland and Kevin McLaughlin, Cambridge, MA, 1999, 220.
2. See Ortrud Westheider's essay in this catalog, 20–29.
3. On this, see especially Hamburg 2004.

Full of Expectation:
Paintings of Children
Ortrud Westheider
pages 170–73

1. See Ellen Key, *The Century of the Child,* trans. Stanton A. Friedberg, New York and London 1909; originally published in Swedish in 1900. See Ulrich Herrmann, "Die 'Majestät des Kindes': Ellen Keys polemische Provokationen," in Ellen Key, *Das Jahrhundert des Kindes,* Weinheim and Basel 1992, 255–66.
2. See Meike Sophia Baader and Juliane Jacobi, "Ellen Keys 'Jahrhundert des Kindes' als pädagogische Programmschrift des 20. Jahrhunderts," in *Kindsein kein Kinderspiel: Das Jahrhundert des Kindes (1900–1999),* exh. cat., Franckesche Stiftungen zu Halle, 2000, 43–52.
3. Sarah Hoke, *Fritz von Uhdes "Kinderstube": Die Darstellung des Kindes in seinem Spiel- und Wohnmilieu,* Göttingen 2011.
4. See *Ein Fest der Künste: Paul Cassirer, der Kunsthändler als Verleger,* exh. cat., Max-Liebermann-Haus, Berlin 2006, 111n37.
5. Sabine Lepsius, "Über Porträtmalerei," in *Deutsche Rundschau Berlin* (March 1941), 141. Unless otherwise noted, all translations are by Steven Lindberg.
6. See Greg M. Thomas, *Impressionist Children: Childhood, Family, and Modern Identity in French Art,* New Haven, CT, 2010; *Great Expectations: John Singer Sargent Painting Children,* exh. cat., Brooklyn Museum, New York 2004.
7. See Berlin 2024a.

The Liberation of Color:
Still Life
Daniel Zamani
pages 188–91

1. Liebermann's collection also included three other still lifes by Édouard Manet, as well as Pierre-Auguste Renoir's *Flowers in a Greenhouse* (1864, Hamburger Kunsthalle) and Gustave Courbet's *Still Life with Apples and Pears* (1871, private collection).

Theatricality:
Big Emotions on Stage and on Canvas
Ortrud Westheider
Seite 206–09

1 In this work, an exception in his oeuvre, Liebermann was reacting to theater and opera performances and poetry from the beginning of the century in which the battle of the sexes is a theme, as in Oscar Wilde's *Salome,* the eponymous opera by Richard Strauss, Friedrich Hebbel's tragedy *Judith,* and Frank Wedekind's dramatic poem *Simson, oder Scham und Eifersucht* (Samson, or Shame and Jealousy).

2 See Hannover 1999, 59.

3 See Barbara Martin, "Wehrhafte Helden, sinnliche Verführerinnen: Das Geschlechterverhältnis bei Corinth," in Hannover 2017, 40–55, here 44.

4 After Édouard Manet's painting *The Dead Christ* of 1864 (Metropolitan Museum of Art, New York), French Impressionist painting rejected Biblical and mythological motifs. By contrast, themes such as the stage and dance were omnipresent in the pictorial world of the Impressionists. But while Edgar Degas saw the theater as a place of social interaction, with ballet rehearsals, views from loges, and events in the orchestra pit (fig. p. 208), artists in Germany focused on stars of the stage and continued a genre that had existed since the Baroque: the role portrait. Biblical themes were also encouraged by Impressionism's great promoter in Germany: Paul Cassirer. He asked Corinth for illustrations for the Pan-Presse for *Judith* in 1909 and for *Das Hohe Lied* (The Song of Songs) in 1910. See Angelika Wesenberg, "'Prachtvolle Erzählungen findet man im Alten Testament': Judith, Simson, Delila um 1900," in *Ein Fest der Künste: Paul Cassirer, der Kunsthändler als Verleger,* exh. cat., Max Liebermann Haus, Berlin 2006, 151–64.

5 In 1899 Paul and Bruno Cassirer exhibited Slevogt's work together with paintings by Édouard Manet. See Bernhard Echte and Walter Feilchenfeldt, *Kunstsalon Cassirer,* vol. 1: *Kunstsalon Bruno & Paul Cassirer: Die Ausstellungen, 1898–1901; "Das Beste aus aller Welt zeigen,"* Wädenswil 2011, 179–214. Slevogt's role portraits found inspiration in Manet's painting of bass baritone *Jean-Baptiste Faure in the Opera "Hamlet" by Ambroise Thomas* (fig. p. 54).

6 See Dominik Brabant, "Welt als Bühne: Theatralität und Performanz in der Malerei Max Slevogts," in Wedekind 2016, 109–14.

7 See Carola Schenk, "Max Slevogt und das Theater: Die Entwicklung des Schauspieler-Rollenportraits," in Wuppertal 2005b, 148–49.

8 See Erika Fischer-Lichte, *Ästhetik des Performativen* [2004], Frankfurt am Main 2014, 42.

9 It survives only in a black-and-white photograph. See *Tänzerinnen um Max Slevogt,* exh. cat., Schloss Villa Ludwigshöhe, Edenkoben 2007, 54.

10 See Sigrun Paas, "Bewegung nach Musik als Motiv," in Chemnitz 2011, 19–21.

11 On Corinth's stage designs for *Salome,* see *Das Theater: Kommentierte Faksimileausgabe der beiden erschienenen Jahrgänge 1903/04–1904/05,* ed. Christian Morgenstern, Emsdetten 1981, 22, 25.

12 See Sarah Elizabeth Jackson, "Embodied Femmes Fatales: Performing Judith and Salomé on the Modernist German Stage," in *Women in German Yearbook* 31 (2015), 48–72, here 55, 65.

Paradise on the Wannsee:
Liebermann's Garden
Daniel Zamani
pages 224–27

1 Quoted in Jenns Eric Howoldt, "Der Nutzgarten: 'Hundert Bilder könnte man hier malen . . . ,'" in Hamburg 2004, 63–64, here 64.

2 Matthias Mühling, "Gartenbänke und Heckengärten," in ibid., 115–16, here 115.

List of Exhibited Works

1
Max Liebermann (1847–1935)
Nursery—Pigpen, 1888
Oil on canvas, 65.5 × 81 cm
Private collection, Germany
Exhibited in Potsdam only

2
Gotthardt Kuehl (1850–1915)
Northern German Hall with Woman Peeling Potatoes, 1885–90
Oil on wood, 65.4 × 52 cm
Galerie von Negelein

3
Max Liebermann (1847–1935)
Tranquil Work, 1885
Oil on canvas, 69 × 46 cm
Museum Kunst der Westküste, Alkersum/Föhr
Inv. 2 LIE 04

4
Fritz von Uhde (1848–1911)
Dutch Sewing Room, 1882
Oil on canvas, 101.5 × 136.5 cm
Private collection

5
Fritz von Uhde (1848–1911)
The Hurdy-Gurdy Man Is Coming, 1883
Oil on canvas, 90 × 151 cm
Hamburger Kunsthalle,
gift of Gustav Diederichsen, 1912
Inv. HK-1636

6
Max Liebermann (1847–1935)
The Garden of the Amsterdam Orphanage, 1894
Oil on canvas, 117 × 152.5 cm
Musée d'Art moderne et contemporain
de Strasbourg
Inv. 55.974.0.680

7
Max Liebermann (1847–1935)
Free Period in the Amsterdam Orphanage, 1881–82
Oil on canvas, 78.5 × 107.5 cm
Städel Museum, Frankfurt am Main,
property of Städelscher Museums-Verein e.V.
Inv. 1351
Exhibited in Potsdam only

8
Gotthardt Kuehl (1850–1915)
Lübeck Orphanage, 1894
Oil on canvas, 87 × 131 cm
Lübecker Museen. Museum Behnhaus
Drägerhaus

9
Gotthardt Kuehl (1850–1915)
Orphans in Lübeck, 1884
Oil on canvas, 98 × 125 cm
Albertinum, Staatliche Kunstsammlungen
Dresden
Inv. 3023

10
Max Liebermann (1847–1935)
Pig Market in Haarlem (First Version), 1890–91
Oil on canvas, 111 × 151 cm
Kunsthalle Mannheim
Inv. M287

11
Max Liebermann (1847–1935)
Pig Market in Haarlem (Second Version), 1894
Oil on canvas, 113.5 × 151.5 cm
Hessisches Landesmuseum Darmstadt
Inv. GK 1101

12
Max Liebermann (1847–1935)
Jewish Street in Amsterdam, 1909
Oil on canvas, 125 × 175 cm
Private collection BRENNET GmbH

13
Max Liebermann (1847–1935)
Vegetable Market in Delft, 1907
Oil on canvas, 71 × 89 cm
Private collection, Berlin

14
Friedrich Kallmorgen (1856–1924)
Tableware Market, 1887
Oil on canvas, 127 × 210 cm
Kunsthalle Mannheim
Inv. M184

15
Friedrich Kallmorgen (1856–1924)
Bright Winter Day, 1881
Oil on canvas, 75 × 60 cm
Private collection
Exhibited in Baden-Baden only

16
Max Liebermann (1847–1935)
Saint Steven's Poorhouse in Leiden (Second Version), 1890
Oil on canvas, 78 × 101 cm
Private collection

17
Max Liebermann (1847–1935)
Hospital Garden in Edam, 1904
Oil on canvas, 70.5 × 88.5 cm
Belvedere, Vienna
Inv. 629

18
Max Liebermann (1847–1935)
Harvest Field, 1912
Oil on canvas, 50 × 68 cm
Staatliche Kunsthalle Karlsruhe
Inv. 1514
Exhibited in Baden-Baden only

19
Maria Slavona (1865–1931)
Landscape near the Oise, 1901–06
Oil on wood, 33 × 41 cm
Lübecker Museen. Museum Behnhaus Drägerhaus
Exhibited in Potsdam only

20
Christian Rohlfs (1849–1938)
The Sternbrücke in Weimar, 1892
Oil on canvas, 61 × 82.5 cm
Museum für Kunst und Kulturgeschichte Schloss Gottorf, Landesmuseen Schleswig-Holstein
Inv 1990-288
Exhibited in Potsdam only

21
Lovis Corinth (1858–1925)
Thriving Cottage Garden, 1904
Oil on canvas, 76 × 100 cm
Museum Wiesbaden
Inv. MUWI-KS-M-0283
Exhibited in Potsdam only

22
Konrad von Kardorff (1877–1945)
Königin-Augusta-Strasse at Calandrelli-Platz in Berlin, 1911
Oil on canvas, 77 × 94 cm
Stiftung Stadtmuseum Berlin
Inv. GEM 72/10

23
Max Liebermann (1847–1935)
Strollers in the Tiergarten, ca. 1927
Oil on wood, 33 × 44 cm
Private collection
Exhibited in Potsdam only

24
Max Liebermann (1847–1935)
Beer Garden in Laren, 1903
Oil on canvas, 71.5 × 101 cm
Private collection

25
Max Liebermann (1847–1935)
Colomierstrasse in Wannsee, 1917
Oil on canvas, 74 × 92 cm
Private collection

26
Max Liebermann (1847–1935)
De Oude Vink Beer Garden near Leiden, 1905
Oil on canvas, 71 × 88 cm
Kunsthaus Zürich, 1925
Inv. 1653
Exhibited in Potsdam only

27
Max Uth (1863–1914)
The Beer Garden, ca. 1910
Oil on canvas, 75.5 × 85 cm
Staatliche Museen zu Berlin, Nationalgalerie
Inv. A II 8

28
Max Liebermann (1847–1935)
Beer Garden in Brannenburg, 1893
Oil on canvas, 70 × 100.2 cm
Musée d'Orsay, Paris,
Acquired from Max Liebermann 1894
Inv. RF 1977 227

29
Max Liebermann (1847–1935)
Beer Garden on the Havel Under the Trees, 1920–22
Oil on canvas, 54.5 × 75 cm
Private collection

30
Max Liebermann (1847–1935)
Beer Garden on the Havel Under the Trees, 1920–22
Oil on canvas, 43 × 65.5 cm
Private collection

31
Max Slevogt (1868–1932)
Group of Horsemen in the Forest, 1902
Oil on canvas, 67.5 × 50.5 cm
Private collection

32
Max Liebermann (1847–1935)
Two Horsemen on the Road near Sakrow, 1924
Oil on canvas, 60 × 75 cm
Galerie Bastian, Berlin
Exhibited in Baden-Baden only

33
Max Liebermann (1847–1935)
Horseman and Horsewoman on the Beach, 1903
Oil on canvas, 72.5 × 101 cm
Wallraf-Richartz-Museum & Fondation Corboud, Cologne
Inv. WRM 2819
Exhibited in Potsdam only

34
Max Liebermann (1847–1935)
Two Horsemen on the Beach Facing Left, ca. 1910
Oil on canvas, 70 × 100.5 cm
Museum Kunst der Westküste, Alkersum/Föhr
Inv. 3 LIE 01

35
Max Liebermann (1847–1935)
Summer Evening on the Alster, 1909
Oil on canvas, 70.5 × 89 cm
Leopold-Hoesch-Museum, Düren
Inv. 1954/1325

36
Christian Landenberger (1862–1927)
Summer Evening at the Lake, 1904
Oil on canvas, 115 × 141 cm
Bayerische Staatsgemäldesammlungen, Munich—Neue Pinakothek
Inv. 8379

37
Max Liebermann (1847–1935)
Beach Life, 1916
Oil on canvas, 66 × 80 cm
Private collection
Exhibited in Potsdam only

38
Lovis Corinth (1858–1925)
On the Baltic Shore, 1903
Oil on canvas, 99.5 × 75 cm
Private collection
Exhibited in Potsdam only

39
Max Liebermann (1847–1935)
On the Beach at Noordwijk, 1908
Oil on canvas, 65.5 × 79,5 cm
Von der Heydt-Museum Wuppertal
Inv. G 1123

40
Max Liebermann (1847–1935)
On the Beach at Noordwijk, 1908
Oil on canvas, 46.5 × 62 cm
Staatliche Kunsthalle Karlsruhe
Inv. 2796

41
Max Liebermann (1847–1935)
After Bathing, 1904
Oil on canvas, 62.9 × 91.1 cm
Tate, bequeathed by G. L. Tietz 1980
Inv. T03077
Exhibited in Potsdam only

42
Philipp Franck (1860–1944)
Wannsee, 1915
Oil on canvas, 81 × 89.3 cm
Private collection, Frankfurt am Main

43
Philipp Franck (1860–1944)
Boys Swimming, 1911
Oil on canvas, 100 × 85 cm
Private collection

44
Lovis Corinth (1858–1925)
Neuer See in the Tiergarten in Berlin, 1908
Oil on canvas, 76 × 100.5 cm
Kunsthalle Mannheim
Inv. M1098

45
Max Liebermann (1847–1935)
Ice Skaters in the Tiergarten, 1921
Oil on canvas, 49 × 53 cm
Private collection, Berlin

46
Lovis Corinth (1858–1925)
Ice Rink in the Tiergarten in Berlin, 1909
Oil on canvas, 66 × 92 cm
Hegenbarth Collection Berlin

47
Max Slevogt (1868–1932)
Unter den Linden (Flags in Berlin), 1913
Oil on canvas, 49 × 57.5 cm
Hessisches Landesmuseum Darmstadt
Inv. GK 609

48
Max Liebermann (1847–1935)
Parrot Man, 1901
Oil on canvas, 85 × 63.5 cm
Private collection
Exhibited in Potsdam only

49
Eva Stort (1855–1936)
View from the Window (Schöneberg), 1890
Oil on canvas, 83 × 110 cm
David Ragusa Collection
Exhibited in Baden-Baden only

50
Lovis Corinth (1858–1925)
Garden in Berlin-Westend, 1925
Oil on canvas, 80 × 100 cm
Von der Heydt-Museum Wuppertal
Inv. G 1195

51
Lovis Corinth (1858–1925)
Unter den Linden, 1922
Oil on canvas, 70.5 × 90 cm
Von der Heydt-Museum Wuppertal
Inv. G 0795

52
Gotthardt Kuehl (1850–1915)
View of Dresden with the Augustus Bridge at Night, ca. 1900
Oil on canvas, 60 × 100 cm
Kunstforum Ostdeutsche Galerie, Regensburg, long-term loan from the KfW Bankengruppe
Inv. 14322
Exhibited in Potsdam only

53
Lesser Ury (1861–1931)
Street at Night in the Rain (Berlin), ca. 1898–1900
Oil on canvas, 52 × 36 cm
Private collection
Exhibited in Baden-Baden only

54
Lesser Ury (1861–1931)
Bellevuestrasse, Berlin, 1912
Oil on canvas, 81.5 × 61 cm
Private collection

55
Lesser Ury (1861–1931)
Nocturnal Street Scene, Berlin—Leipziger Strasse, ca. 1915–20
Oil on canvas, 51.2 × 36.2 cm
Private collection

56
Lesser Ury (1861–1931)
Café König at Night (Unter den Linden), 1925–30
Oil on canvas, 105 × 68 cm
Private collection, southern Germany
Exhibited in Potsdam only

57
Lesser Ury (1861–1931)
Elevated Subway Station at Bülowstrasse, 1922
Oil on canvas, 70 × 100.5 cm
Private collection, southern Germany
Exhibited in Potsdam only

58
Lesser Ury (1861–1931)
Carriages (Rainy Atmosphere), 1916
Oil on canvas, 59 × 45 cm
Private collection

59
Lesser Ury (1861–1931)
Nocturnal Street Scene, Berlin, ca. 1915–20
Oil on canvas, 78 × 60.5 cm
Dr. Matthias Wilkening Foundation

60
Lesser Ury (1861–1931)
Woman and Man in a Café, 1920s
Oil on canvas, 27.4 × 36 cm
Private collection

61
Lesser Ury (1861–1931)
Woman and Man, Unter den Linden, 1889
Oil on canvas, 105.3 × 59.3 cm
Private collection, southern Germany
Exhibited in Potsdam only

62
Max Liebermann (1847–1935)
Concert at the Opera, 1922
Oil on canvas, 38.5 × 50.5 cm
Arp Museum Bahnhof Rolandseck, courtesy private collection, Cologne
Exhibited in Potsdam only

63
Lesser Ury (1861–1931)
Café de la Paix at Night, Paris, 1928
Oil on canvas on cardboard, 23.7 × 32.5 cm
Private collection, southern Germany

64
Lovis Corinth (1858–1925)
Woman Reading, 1911
Oil on canvas, 45 × 70 cm
Private collection

65
Lovis Corinth (1858–1925)
Morning Sun, 1910
Oil on canvas, 68.5 × 80.5 cm
Hessisches Landesmuseum Darmstadt
Inv. GK 1144

66
Lovis Corinth (1858–1925)
Woman at the Goldfish Tank, 1911
Oil on canvas, 74 × 90.5 cm
Belvedere, Vienna
Inv. 1829

67
Emilie von Hallavanya (1874–1960)
Self-Portrait, 1905 (?)
Oil on canvas, 101.1 × 84 cm
Städtische Galerie im Lenbachhaus und Kunstbau, Munich
Inv. G 3971
Exhibited in Potsdam only

68
Lovis Corinth (1858–1925)
Christmas Tree (Distributing Presents), 1913
Oil on canvas, 120 × 80.5 cm
Lentos Kunstmuseum Linz
Inv. 71

69
Franz Skarbina (1849–1910)
Christmas Room, Berlin, 1892
Oil on canvas, 75 × 60.5 cm
Stiftung Stadtmuseum Berlin
Inv. GEM 68/24

70
Wilhelm Trübner (1851–1917)
Girl in a Tree, 1907
Oil on canvas, 71.5 × 57 cm
Kurpfälzisches Museum Heidelberg
Inv. G 2540
Exhibited in Baden-Baden only

71
Ludwig von Gleichen-Russwurm (1836–1901)
Stroll Under Flowering Apple Trees, 1893
Oil on canvas, 86 × 129 cm
Museum im Kulturspeicher, Würzburg

72
Philipp Franck (1860–1944)
Wannsee Garden (Rose Arbor in the Arnholds' Garden), 1919
Oil on canvas, 125 × 125 cm
Private collection
Exhibited in Baden-Baden only

73
Lovis Corinth (1858–1925)
Flowering Apple Tree, 1922
Oil on canvas, 70 × 90.4 cm
Private collection
Exhibited in Potsdam only

74
Max Slevogt (1868–1932)
Garden Path to the Summer House (Godramstein), 1912
Oil on canvas, 61.8 × 77.5 cm
Private collection

75
Max Slevogt (1868–1932)
The Hollyhock Gardener, 1920
Oil on canvas, 98 × 66.5 cm
Kunsthalle Mannheim
Inv. M498

76
Max Slevogt (1868–1932)
Children at the Pond (Garden in Godramstein), 1909
Oil on canvas, 63 × 78.5 cm
Private collection
Exhibited in Baden-Baden only

77
Max Slevogt (1868–1932)
Gardener in Front of the House, 1910
Oil on canvas, 78 × 62.5 cm
Private collection
Exhibited in Baden-Baden only

78
Max Slevogt (1868–1932)
Bathing Boys, 1911
Oil on canvas, 80 × 102 cm
Belvedere, Vienna
Inv. 2826

79
Max Slevogt (1868–1932)
House in Godramstein—Wolfgang with Goat, 1909
Oil on canvas, 75.6 × 62.1 cm
Private collection
Exhibited in Baden-Baden only

80
MAX SLEVOGT (1868–1932)
Portrait of Suzanne Aimée Cassirer, 1901
Oil on canvas, 100 × 150 cm
Private collection

81
MAX SLEVOGT (1868–1932)
Nina as an Indian, 1913
Oil on canvas, 100 × 80.5 cm
GDKE—Direktion Landesmuseum Mainz
Inv. SL 92

82
HEINRICH EDUARD LINDE-WALTHER (1868–1939)
Child in a Playroom, 1901
Oil on canvas, 123 × 93.5 cm
Lübecker Museen. Museum Behnhaus Drägerhaus

83
FRITZ VON UHDE (1848–1911)
The Garden Path, 1903
Oil on canvas, 61 × 76 cm
Kunsthalle Bremen—Der Kunstverein in Bremen
Inv. 279-1904/23

84
FRITZ VON UHDE (1848–1911)
The Lesson, 1899
Oil on canvas, 88.5 × 111 cm
Museum Folkwang, Essen
Inv. G 192

85
SABINE LEPSIUS (1864–1942)
Portrait of a Child (Margarete Catharina Litten), 1895
Oil on canvas, 134 × 69.5 cm (framed)
Staatliche Museen zu Berlin, Nationalgalerie
Inv. NG/7 09

86
SABINE LEPSIUS (1864–1942)
Monica, the Artist's Daughter, 1900
Oil on canvas, 93 × 75 cm
Staatliche Museen zu Berlin, Nationalgalerie
Inv. A II 958

87
FRITZ VON UHDE (1848–1911)
Children's Room, 1889
Oil on canvas, 110.7 × 138.5 cm
Hamburger Kunsthalle, gift of Alfred Beit, 1901
Inv. HK-1637

88
CHARLOTTE BEREND-CORINTH (1880–1967)
Henny (Henriette Seckbach), 1905
Oil on canvas, 100.2 × 61.1 cm
Städtische Galerie im Lenbachhaus und Kunstbau, Munich
Inv. G 15433
Exhibited in Potsdam only

89
DORA HITZ (1856–1924)
Portrait of a Small Girl, before 1897
Oil on canvas, 100.5 × 73 cm
Staatliche Museen zu Berlin, Nationalgalerie
Inv. A I 580

90
SABINE LEPSIUS (1864–1942)
Girl in Sunday Dress, 1914
Pastel on canvas, 113 × 87 cm
David Ragusa Collection

91
SABINE LEPSIUS (1864–1942)
Double Portrait of the Sisters Cornelia (Born in 1921) and Charlotte Hahn (Born in 1926), 1932
Oil on canvas, 80.5 × 85.5 cm
Jüdisches Museum Berlin
Inv. GEM 96/3/0

92
MAX SLEVOGT (1868–1932)
Still Life with Chocolate Rabbits, 1923
Oil on canvas, 59 × 79 cm
GDKE—Direktion Landesmuseum Mainz
Inv. LHS 01/1

93
MAX SLEVOGT (1868–1932)
Summer Flowers, 1928
Oil on canvas, 65 × 44.6 cm
Private collection, courtesy Daxer & Marschall, Munich

94
MAX SLEVOGT (1868–1932)
Red Carnations, 1904
Oil on canvas, 78.5 × 62.5 cm
Private collection

95
MARIA SLAVONA (1865–1931)
Still Life with Red Background, 1911
Oil on canvas, 80.5 × 100 cm
Stiftung Schlösschen im Hofgarten Wertheim

96
GEORG BURMESTER (1864–1936)
Bouquet of Summer Flowers, 1911
Oil on canvas, 64 × 50 cm
Galerie von Negelein
Exhibited in Baden-Baden only

97
MAX SLEVOGT (1868–1932)
Still Life with Eggs and Citrus Fruits, 1925
Oil on canvas, 55.5 × 70.5 cm
Private collection
Exhibited in Baden-Baden only

98
MAX SLEVOGT (1868–1932)
Fruit Still Life, 1911
Oil on canvas, 61 × 80 cm
Staatliche Kunsthalle Karlsruhe
Inv. 1544

99
MAX SLEVOGT (1868–1932)
Still Life with Apples, Grapes, and Plums, 1914
Oil on canvas, 75 × 84 cm
Private collection
Exhibited in Baden-Baden only

100
LOVIS CORINTH (1858–1925)
Yellow and Red Asters, 1921
Oil on canvas, 100 × 80 cm
Galerie Paffrath

101
Lovis Corinth (1858–1925)
Flower Still Life (Calla Lilies and Lilacs with Bronze Figure), 1920
Oil on canvas, 120 × 125 cm
Von der Heydt-Museum Wuppertal
Inv. G 0228

102
Lesser Ury (1861–1931)
Bouquet of Lilacs, 1922
Oil on canvas, 101.5 × 70 cm
Staatliche Museen zu Berlin, Nationalgalerie
Inv. A II 403

103
Heinrich Hübner (1869–1945)
Larkspurs, 1913
Oil on canvas, 90.2 × 80.3 cm
Staatliche Museen zu Berlin, Nationalgalerie
Inv. A II 376

104
Max Liebermann (1847–1935)
Self-Portrait, 1934
Oil on canvas, 92.1 × 73.3 cm
Tate, presented by Lord Marks 1935
Inv. N04779
Exhibited in Potsdam only

105
Max Liebermann (1847–1935)
Self-Portrait in Suit at the Easel, 1922
Oil on canvas, 90 × 75.3 cm
Galerie Bastian, Berlin
Exhibited in Baden-Baden only

106
Lovis Corinth (1858–1925)
Julius Meier-Graefe, 1912
Oil on canvas, 90 × 70 cm
Musée d'Orsay, Paris, Gift E. J. Goeritz, 1936
Inv. RF 1977 109

107
Lovis Corinth (1858–1925)
Woman with Wineglass, 1918
Oil on canvas, 73 × 53 cm
Von der Heydt-Museum Wuppertal
Inv. G 1182

108
Lovis Corinth (1858–1925)
Portrait of Mrs. Douglas (Irma Hübner), 1909
Oil on canvas, 140 × 100 cm
Museum der bildenden Künste Leipzig
Inv. G 1259

109
Max Slevogt (1868–1932)
Dancer in Gold, 1895
Oil on canvas, 78.5 × 65.5 cm
GDKE—Direktion Landesmuseum Mainz
Inv. SL 59

110
Max Slevogt (1868–1932)
Dancer in Silver, 1895
Oil on canvas, 78 × 64.5 cm
GDKE—Direktion Landesmuseum Mainz
Inv. 76/217

111
Max Liebermann (1847–1935)
Samson and Delilah, 1902
Oil on canvas, 151.1 × 212 cm
Städel Museum, Frankfurt am Main, purchased in 1910
Inv. SG 171

112
Lovis Corinth (1858–1925)
Gertrud Eysoldt as Salome, 1903
Oil on canvas, 108.5 × 84 cm
Klassik Stiftung Weimar, Museen; acquired with funds from Bauhaus.Weimar. Moderne. Die Kunstfreunde and the Federal Republic of Germany (joint ownership)
Inv. G 2414

113
Max Slevogt (1868–1932)
The Abduction, 1905
Oil on canvas, 181.5 × 131 cm
Niedersächsisches Landesmuseum Hannover
Inv. KM Slg. Wrede I, 14
Exhibited in Potsdam only

114
Max Slevogt (1868–1932)
D'Andrade in Black, 1903
Oil on canvas, 150 × 109 cm
Hamburger Kunsthalle, purchased in 1969
Inv. HK-5149

115
Max Slevogt (1868–1932)
The Champagne Aria, 1902
Oil on canvas, 215 × 160 cm
Staatsgalerie Stuttgart, purchased from the artist in 1904
Inv. 1123

116
Max Slevogt (1868–1932)
Singer Francisco d'Andrade as Don Giovanni in Mozart's Opera, 1912
Oil on canvas, 210 × 170 cm
Staatliche Museen zu Berlin, Nationalgalerie
Inv. A II 36

117
Max Liebermann (1847–1935)
The Artist's Granddaughter with Her Governess in the Wannsee Garden, 1923
Oil on canvas, 75.7 × 100 cm
Museo Nacional Thyssen-Bornemisza, Carmen Thyssen Collection, Madrid
Inv. CTB.1993.6
Exhibited in Potsdam only

118
Max Liebermann (1847–1935)
The Kitchen Garden in Wannsee to the Southeast, 1923
Oil on canvas, 55 × 76 cm
Private collection

119
Max Liebermann (1847–1935)
The Kitchen Garden in Wannsee to the Northwest, 1923
Oil on canvas, 55 × 75 cm
Private collection

120
Max Liebermann (1847–1935)
Perennials at the Gardener's House to the Northeast, 1926
Oil on canvas, 54 × 75.2 cm
Private collection, Cologne, courtesy Galerie Paffrath

121
Max Liebermann (1847–1935)
Wannsee Garden—House with Red Perennials, 1926
Oil on canvas, 54 × 76 cm
Galerie Bastian, Berlin
Exhibited in Baden-Baden only

122
Max Liebermann (1847–1935)
Perennials at the Gardener's House to the East, 1923
Oil on canvas, 55.5 × 75.5 cm
Private collection

123
Max Liebermann (1847–1935)
Perennials in the Kitchen Garden to the Southwest, 1926
Oil on canvas, 71.5 × 94.5 cm
Private collection, courtesy Lempertz, Cologne
Exhibited in Baden-Baden only

124
Max Liebermann (1847–1935)
The Flowerbeds in the Wannsee Garden to the Northwest, 1916
Oil on canvas, 59.5 × 89.5 cm
Kunstmuseum Solothurn, Dübi-Müller-Stiftung
Inv. C 80.20

125
Max Liebermann (1847–1935)
The Flowerbeds in the Wannsee Garden to the Northwest, 1921
Oil on canvas, 50.3 × 75 cm
Kunstmuseum Gelsenkirchen
Inv. C80.20

126
Max Liebermann (1847–1935)
The Flowerbeds in the Wannsee Garden to the South, 1921
Oil on canvas, 48.5 × 70.5 cm
Private collection

127
Max Liebermann (1847–1935)
Garden Bench Under the Chestnut Tree—Flowering Chestnuts, 1916
Oil on canvas, 70 × 90 cm
Private collection

128
Max Liebermann (1847–1935)
The Birch Path in the Wannsee Garden to the Southwest, 1924
Oil on canvas, 50.6 × 70.2 cm
Kunstsammlungen Chemnitz
Inv. 171

129
Max Liebermann (1847–1935)
The Kitchen Garden in Wannsee to the Northeast—Perennials, 1916
Oil on canvas, 40 × 50 cm
Private collection
Exhibited in Baden-Baden only

130
Max Liebermann (1847–1935)
The Kitchen Garden in Wannsee to the West, with a Gardener on the Path, ca. 1924
Oil on wood, 61 × 75 cm
Private collection

131
Max Liebermann (1847–1935)
My House in Wannsee with the Garden, ca. 1926
Oil on canvas, 70.5 × 90.2 cm
Private collection

132
Max Liebermann (1847–1935)
Perennials in Front of the Gardener's House to the North, 1928
Oil on canvas, 73 × 91.5 cm
Private collection

Christiane Righetti

Chronology

Max Liebermann and Impressionism in Germany, 1870–1935

1870

The Franco-Prussian War begins on July 19 and continues until May 10, 1871, ending in a devastating defeat for France. Max Liebermann, who serves as a volunteer medic in the war, is deeply shaken by his experiences on the front. During the military conflict, France becomes a republic, while the German states unite into an empire under the aegis of Prussia. The city of Berlin, formerly the residence of the Prussian kings, becomes the capital of the empire and in subsequent years develops into a burgeoning modern metropolis. In the decades to follow, ongoing political tensions between Germany and France continue to pose obstacles for artistic and cultural exchange.

1871

Liebermann makes his first journey to Holland, where he will later paint for extended periods of time. During his travels he meets Hungarian artist Mihály Munkácsy, whose large-scale painting *Woman Making Lint* (1871, Szépművészeti Múzeum / Museum of Fine Arts, Budapest) inspires Liebermann's first major work, *Women Plucking Geese* (1871–72, Alte Nationalgalerie, Berlin). Liebermann's painting is exhibited in 1872, first in Hamburg and then in Berlin. The dark-toned image of laboring women garners him the derogatory epithet *Schmutzmaler* (painter of dirt). In 1874 this painting would mark his debut at the Salon in Paris.

1872

Liebermann makes his first trip to the French capital. Galerie Bernheim-Jeune in Paris shows active interest in his work, and through the gallery he is able to sell two paintings to private collectors in France.

1873

After completing his studies at the Academy of Art in Weimar, the twenty-six-year-old Liebermann returns to Paris. Despite the tense political atmosphere of the postwar years, he spends five years in the French metropolis, studying works of modern French art and the new plein-air painting. In the Louvre, he also copies seventeenth-century Dutch paintings.

1
Max Liebermann,
Potato Harvest, 1875,
Kunstpalast Düsseldorf

2
Max Liebermann,
The Old Men's Home in Amsterdam, 1880,
Museum Georg Schäfer, Schweinfurt

1874

From April 15 to May 15, the first of the eight Impressionist exhibitions takes place in Paris. The show is organized by the participating artists themselves—including Paul Cézanne, Edgar Degas, Claude Monet, Berthe Morisot, Camille Pissarro, and Pierre-Auguste Renoir—in self-confident competition with the official Salon. The exhibition is considered a breakthrough for Impressionism, which had emerged in Paris in the early 1860s from Realist tendencies. This new painterly approach, marked by luminous color and the sketch-like rendering of objects, soon extends beyond the borders of France and, from the 1880s on, also influences the development of modern art in Germany.

Together with artists Carl Fredrik Hill and László Paál, Liebermann spends the summer at the artists' colony in Barbizon studying plein-air painting. He is impressed by the Realism of Gustave Courbet as well as that of Jean-François Millet, whose work inspires him to paint the *Potato Harvest* (fig. 1), a rural scene focusing on the hard labor of the peasants.

1875

In the spring of 1875, Liebermann and Hill go to Barbizon together for the last time. Thereafter, Liebermann embarks on his own exploration of Holland, where he will stay for months at a time in subsequent years. He is especially interested in the motif of girls sewing. The next year, he makes the first studies for the painting *Free Period in the Amsterdam Orphanage* (cat. 7), which portrays children in the inner courtyard of an orphanage founded in 1520.

1879

Liebermann's first history painting, *The Twelve-Year-Old Jesus in the Temple* (1879, Hamburger Kunsthalle), provokes a scandal at the *Internationale Kunst-Ausstellung* (International Art Exhibition) in Munich. Conservative critics see it as an attack on Christianity, since it shows Jesus as a dirty street urchin in a realistic, everyday setting.

During his time in Munich, Liebermann meets painter Fritz von Uhde, whom he introduces to plein-air painting. At Liebermann's recommendation, Uhde later travels to Holland and visits places including Zandvoort, where he creates the studies for the painting *The Hurdy-Gurdy Man Is Coming* (cat. 5) in the late summer of 1882.

Gotthardt Kuehl moves into a studio in the ninth arrondissement in Paris, which is frequented by numerous younger artists. Beginning the following year, Kuehl, Uhde, and Liebermann regularly exhibit at the Paris Salon.

1880

Fritz Gurlitt opens his gallery in Berlin, offering a forum to anti-academic artists such as Wilhelm Leibl, Max Liebermann, Franz Skarbina, Wilhelm Trübner, and Lesser Ury.

During a stay in Amsterdam, a home for old men inspires Liebermann to create one of his most important early Impressionist works (fig. 2). Here for the first time, he uses patches of sunlight as a central painterly motif to evoke a sense of immediacy and dynamism. Paintings such as *The Old Men's Home in Amsterdam* as well as the thematically related *Free Period in the Amsterdam Orphanage*, completed in 1882, establish Liebermann's mature Impressionist style. Although he uses plein-air sketches to capture the scenes on location, unlike the French Impressionists, he executes the finished paintings in the studio.

3
W. von Debschitz-Kunowski,
Martha Liebermann in the Wannsee garden, 1927

1881

At the Salon, the jury awards an honorable mention to Liebermann's painting *The Old Men's Home in Amsterdam*. He is the first German painter after the Franco-Prussian War to receive this distinction, and as a result also attracts the attention of French collectors.

1882

The first important German collectors of French Impressionism, Carl and Felicie Bernstein in Berlin, acquire paintings from Paris by artists such as Édouard Manet, Claude Monet, Camille Pissarro, and Alfred Sisley. The following year, ten of these works are shown at the first exhibition of French Impressionism in Germany at the Berlin gallery of Fritz Gurlitt.

1883

In the winter of 1882–83, Fritz von Uhde begins working on a painting based on sketches from Holland as well as a number of pieces of traditional costume brought back from Zandvoort. He completes the large-scale painting *The Hurdy-Gurdy Man Is Coming* (cat. 5), a genre scene that echoes the tradition of what is known as *Bettelromantik* (beggar romanticism). Von Uhde gives the painting to Liebermann in exchange for the latter's *The Twelve-Year-Old Jesus in the Temple.*

1884

4
Max Liebermann,
The Flax Barn at Laren, 1887,
Alte Nationalgalerie, Berlin,
donated by the artist in 1889

After a six-year stay in Munich, Liebermann moves back to Berlin. There, he is introduced to the collection of the Bernsteins who, like him, live in the Tiergarten district.

In September, Liebermann marries Martha Marckwald (fig. 3), his sister-in-law's sister. The couple spends their honeymoon in Holland, where they visit locations including Scheveningen, Laren, Delden, Haarlem, and Amsterdam. In August of the following year, their only child is born, Marianne Henriette Käthe Liebermann, known as Käthe (1885–1952).

The genre painting *Orphans in Lübeck* by Gotthardt Kuehl (cat. 9) is exhibited at the Paris Salon, where it is received with great enthusiasm. The subject of the work echoes Liebermann's orphanage scenes.

1885

Liebermann makes the acquaintance of art historian Alfred Lichtwark, who as director of the Hamburger Kunsthalle will become one of his most important supporters.

1888–89

Friedrich Kallmorgen helps found the painters' colony in Grötzingen. Like the groups in Barbizon and Worpswede, the artists there develop a new approach to landscape painting, in which the focus lies not on a romanticized idyll but on the ordinariness of the scene.

1889

Since the German government refuses to participate in the Exposition Universelle in Paris (May 6–October 31), Liebermann and Gotthardt Kuehl organize a private exhibition of contemporary German art with works by Franz Skarbina, Wilhelm Trübner, Fritz von Uhde, and others.

For his service, the French state awards Liebermann a medal of honor and admits him as one of the first German artists to the prestigious Société des Beaux-Arts. Liebermann and Kuehl are appointed knights of the Legion of Honor by the French government. Since Liebermann is a resident of Berlin, the Prussian government initially prohibits him from accepting the honor; Kuehl, however, who lives in Munich, is allowed to receive it. From among his own works exhibited at the Exposition Universelle, Liebermann gives the painting *Net Menders* (fig. p. 24) to the Hamburger Kunsthalle. Previously, he had also donated *The Flax Barn at Laren* (fig. 4) to the Nationalgalerie in Berlin.

Liebermann spends the summer in Katwijk aan Zee in Holland. During a brief excursion to nearby Leiden, he paints *Saint Steven's Poorhouse in Leiden* (Alte Nationalgalerie, Berlin). During the fall or winter, he creates a second version in the studio (cat. 16).

Kuehl's painting *A Difficult Question* (before 1889, Musée d'Orsay, Paris) is purchased by the Musée du Luxembourg, the first work by a German artist to be acquired after 1871.

1890

5
The Liebermann family's town house at Pariser Platz 7, Berlin (to the right of the Brandenburg Gate), 1892

In the spring, Liebermann makes his first working trip to Hamburg. There, along with Gotthardt Kuehl, he assists Alfred Lichtwark with the project "Collection of Paintings from Hamburg." A lively correspondence begins between the two friends.

At the Academy of Art in Weimar, works by French Impressionists are presented to a wider public for the first time.

1891

Alfred Lichtwark procures for Liebermann his first official portrait commission: *Mayor Carl Friedrich Petersen* (1891, Hamburger Kunsthalle). The portrait, painted in the style of Frans Hals, is criticized for focusing more on the person than on the sitter's official position.

1892

On April 4 the Munich Secession is established in order to provide artists with better exhibition opportunities. Its ninety-six founding members include Lovis Corinth, Gotthardt Kuehl, Max Liebermann, Max Slevogt, and Wilhelm Trübner. The association will play a key role in the rise of the German avant-garde.

On February 5 in Berlin, Liebermann founds the Association of the XI together with Walter Leistikow and other artists who have been rejected by the academy, including Franz Skarbina and later Dora Hitz. Liebermann remains a leading member until the founding of the Berlin Secession and the concomitant dissolution of the XI.

1894

After his father's death, Liebermann inherits the house at Pariser Platz 7 in the immediate vicinity of the Brandenburg Gate, a town house that had belonged to the Liebermann family since 1857 (fig. 5). He resides there with his family in a home on the third floor until his death in 1935. The large inheritance also enables him to develop one of the most important private collections of French Impressionist art worldwide.

Liebermann's 1893 painting *Beer Garden in Brannenburg* (cat. 28) is exhibited at the Paris Salon and is acquired by the French state for the Musée du Luxembourg, a testimony to the artist's reputation in France as a leading modern painter.

6
Wilhelm Schulz (design),
poster of the second exhibition of the Berlin Secession,
1900

1896

In the spring, Liebermann travels to Paris with Hugo von Tschudi, director of the Nationalgalerie in Berlin. Von Tschudi purchases Édouard Manet's painting *In the Conservatory* (ill. p. 22) from Paul Durand-Ruel, the first acquisition of a work of French Impressionism for a German museum collection. During this trip, Liebermann meets Edgar Degas. In 1896 he is finally allowed to accept his invitation into the French Legion of Honor, which the German government had vetoed in 1889.

1897

On his fiftieth birthday, Liebermann becomes a member of the Royal Academy of the Arts in Berlin and is appointed professor, sealing his public recognition. The same year, he receives the long-hoped-for Great Golden Medal from the academy.

1898

Liebermann is elected president of the Berlin Secession, an association of independent artists founded on May 2 to protest the strictures of the academy and the conservative views of the imperial elite. The sixty-five founding members also include women artists Dora Hitz and Sabine Lepsius. On May 19, 1899, the first exhibition of the Secession opens in the building at Kantstrasse 12, which is planned by Hans Grisebach and newly constructed within a short period of time. The show is a resounding success.

Cousins Paul and Bruno Cassirer open their Kunstsalon (art salon) in Berlin. They are appointed executive secretaries of the Secession, garnering them a prominent position in the art market. In the years that follow, they concentrate their efforts as dealers and publishers on promoting the art of Impressionism. Working closely with his French colleague Paul Durand-Ruel, Paul Cassirer gradually brings a large number of the most important works of French Impressionism to Berlin, including Monet's early masterpiece *Impression, Sunrise* in 1899 (fig. p. 23).

1900

The Berlin Secession opens its second exhibition (May–October), now including numerous works by French artists such as Paul Cézanne, Claude Monet, Camille Pissarro, Auguste Rodin, and Alfred Sisley (fig. 6).

1901

In Holland, Liebermann produces his first brilliantly colored, sun-drenched beach scenes with riders and vacationers. The Impressionist painting of light becomes a central theme of his work, which is marked more and more by glowing colors and dynamic brushwork.

Max Slevogt moves to the German capital and soon becomes a member of the Berlin Secession. The same year, he begins work on *The Champagne Aria* (cat. 115), one of three large-scale paintings showing Portuguese baritone Francisco d'Andrade in the role of Don Giovanni in the eponymous 1787 Mozart opera. He is able to draw inspiration for these theatrical depictions from Édouard Manet's images of French opera singer Jean-Baptiste Faure (figs. pp. 54, 209). Slevogt's fellow artist Lovis Corinth soon also embraces the new pictorial type known as the role portrait (see cat. 112).

1902

Bruno Cassirer founds the magazine *Kunst und Künstler* with Emil Heilbut as editor-in-chief. In 1889 Heilbut had shown three works by Claude Monet from his private collection in the context of a lecture at the Grand Ducal Art School in Weimar—to the great enthusiasm of the painters in attendance, as Ludwig von Gleichen-Rußwurm and Christian Rohlfs report.

Liebermann paints *Samson and Delilah* (cat. 111), one of his most ambitious figural works. The emphatically theatrical rendering of the biblical scene recalls the role portraits of Max Slevogt and Lovis Corinth.

1903

Liebermann cofounds the Deutscher Künstlerbund (Association of German Artists) together with Harry Graf Kessler, director of the Grand Ducal Museum of Arts and Crafts in Weimar, and artists such as Lovis Corinth, Max Slevogt, and Wilhelm Trübner. In response to persistent criticism of his art, he publishes the essay "Die Phantasie in der Malerei" ("Imagination in Painting") in the magazine *Neue Rundschau*. Later, in the foreword to the second edition of 1916, he writes:

There is no stupider claim than the one we . . . read and hear daily: that Naturalism is dead. For all art is based on nature, and everything lasting in it is nature. Not only that which surrounds the artist, but above all his own nature. How he, the artist, views the world, with his internal and external senses—I call that his imagination—the forming of this, his imagination, is his art. As a painter, I proceed from vision, and so I am interested exclusively in the forming imagination, while for me the creative imagination in the work of art is an axiom. It is divine inspiration, with which we can come to grips only by way of pure thought (if we can come to grips with it at all). But we may hope to trace the workings of the forming imagination through psychological and empirical means. Or in other words: we are permitted to want to try, through technique, to explain the spirit that engendered the work.

Lovis Corinth marries his student Charlotte Berend, who along with her own artistic activity (cat. 88) also models for him for numerous works (cats. 64–66).

7
Liebermann's Wannsee villa, 1925

8
View of the hedge gardens at Liebermann's Wannsee villa

1904

The German contribution to the world's fair in Saint Louis, in the United States, is still wholly in keeping with Germany's regressive art policy. In response to criticism by Harry Graf Kessler in the magazine *Kunst und Künstler*, the government resolves to consider the interests of the Deutscher Künstlerbund in the future.

Julius Meier-Graefe publishes his *Entwicklungsgeschichte der modernen Kunst* (Developmental History of Modern Art), which is released in English as *Modern Art: Being a Contribution to a New System of Aesthetics* in 1908.

At the *Internationale Kunst-Ausstellung* (International Art Exhibition) in Munich, Christian Landenberger is awarded the Small Golden Medal for his painting *Summer Evening at the Lake* (cat. 36).

1906

Emperor Wilhelm II refuses permission for an exhibition planned by Wilhelm von Bode in celebration of Liebermann's sixtieth birthday. A 1907 retrospective in Liebermann's honor at the Berlin Secession, however, is a great success.

1908

Liebermann spends the summer in the coastal town of Noordwijk in Holland. There, his art dealer Paul Cassirer builds a villa in the dunes to which he invites his artist friends. In numerous beach scenes with bathers, Liebermann captures fleeting impressions of the summer atmosphere (cats. 39, 40).

After the death of Felicie Bernstein, Édouard Manet's 1882 painting *White Lilacs* (fig. p. 33) is bequeathed to the collection of the Nationalgalerie. It later serves as inspiration for Lesser Ury's 1922 still life *Bouquet of Lilacs* (cat. 102).

Due to his acquisition of works by French painters for the Nationalgalerie, Hugo von Tschudi is reprimanded, placed on leave, and eventually dismissed the following year. As director of the Bayerische Staatsgemäldesammlungen in Munich, however, he is able to continue his energetic support of modern French art.

1909

Liebermann acquires a plot of land in the villa colony of Alsen in the Berlin district of Wannsee and commissions architect Paul Otto Baumgarten to build him a house (fig. 7). His friend Alfred Lichtwark assists him with the design of the garden (fig. 8). Between now and 1932, he will paint some two hundred views of the garden from a variety of perspectives (cats. 117–32). For these works, the artist makes no preparatory studies and, like his French counterparts, composes directly on the canvas using the *alla prima* technique.

Thirty years after the initial publication of Théodore Duret's *Les Peintres impressionnistes*, a German translation of the book is published by Bruno Cassirer.

9
Grete Friedländer,
Max Liebermann seated with cigar, ca. 1930

1910–11

Within the Berlin Secession, a public rift develops between the established Impressionists around Max Liebermann and the younger Expressionists around Emil Nolde. After the subsequent founding of the Neue Secession, Liebermann resigns from his position as president of the Berlin Secession the following year. Lovis Corinth is then elected as the new head. In 1911 the Secession organizes an exhibition in honor of deceased member Fritz von Uhde. Lesser Ury, who is embroiled in constant conflict with Liebermann, is now finally able to exhibit at the Secession. Paul Cassirer mounts a highly successful retrospective for Ury with eighty works. Due to ongoing conflicts, Liebermann leaves the Berlin Secession in 1913.

1912

Liebermann is elected to the senate of the Academy of the Arts in Berlin and receives an honorary doctorate from the University of Berlin. He also enjoys international acclaim: he is awarded the Order of Orange-Nassau by the queen of Holland and named a member of the Academy in Stockholm as well as the Académie Française in Paris.

1913

The Berlin Secession shows the largest exhibition of Lovis Corinth's work during his lifetime, with 228 works. The same year, it also mounts a major special exhibition for Wilhelm Trübner.

Liebermann travels to Holland for the last time. In a letter to Alfred Lichtwark from the Hotel Huis ter Duin on August 19, he sums up his final summer in Noordwijk: "For a week now I've once again been here, where I know every person, every house, nearly every tree, where I've painted almost everything." A year later, World War I breaks out, putting an end to Liebermann's regular visits to Holland.

10
Suse Byk,
Max Liebermann's granddaughter, Maria Riezler, in the rose garden at Liebermann's Wannsee villa, ca. 1922, Katharine Whild Estate

11
Max Liebermann,
Granddaughter and Governess Playing in the Garden, 1919, private collection

1914

Max Slevogt acquires the Neukastel estate, known as the Slevogthof. The house and surrounding garden will become a primary focus of his late Impressionist painting (fig. p. 52).

1917

In March, Liebermann's granddaughter, Maria, is born, whom he will often portray in the years to come (figs. 10, 11). In honor of his seventieth birthday, the Royal Academy in Berlin mounts a retrospective exhibition with 191 works.

1920

In October, Liebermann is elected president of Berlin's academy, now known as the Academy of the Arts, an institution he once ardently opposed. He uses his cultural-political influence to promote modern art and a liberal exhibition policy. He is confirmed in this position every year until 1932.

1927

In honor of his eightieth birthday, Max Liebermann receives important national and international accolades. He is made an honorary citizen of Berlin and a major special exhibition is organized for him at the Prussian Academy of the Arts (June–July).

1932

For reasons of age, Liebermann withdraws from the office of president of the academy. His eighty-fifth birthday marks his farewell to public life. He is named honorary president of the Prussian Academy of the Arts.

12
Max Liebermann leaving a polling station after voting for the president of the German Reich, Berlin, March 13, 1932

1933

The Nazi seizure of power on January 30 marks a profound political and cultural caesura. With his resignation from the Prussian Academy of the Arts and the relinquishing of his honorary presidency, Liebermann, a Jew, preemptively forestalls dismissal by the Nazis. He sends major works from his collection of Impressionist paintings to the Kunsthaus Zürich for safekeeping. Today, the works are widely scattered and belong in large part to collections in the United States.

1935

Liebermann dies on February 8 at his house on Pariser Platz in Berlin. He is buried in the family tomb in the Jewish cemetery on Schönhauser Allee. Along with Käthe Kollwitz, Konrad von Kardorff is one of only four artists to pay their final respects to the painter—a consequence of his contempt for the Nazi regime. In 1938 Liebermann's daughter, Käthe, emigrates to New York along with her husband, Kurt Riezler, and twenty-one-year-old daughter, Maria. In 1943 Martha Liebermann commits suicide a few days before her planned deportation to Theresienstadt. In 2006 the Liebermanns' summer home in Wannsee is inaugurated as a museum. Since then, it has served as a cultural memorial, along with the elaborately reconstructed artist's garden (see fig. 7).

Selected Bibliography

Achberg 2021
Lesser Ury: Stadt Land Licht, exh. cat., Schloss Achberg, 2021.

Achenbach 1974
Sigrid Achenbach, *Die Druckgraphik Max Liebermanns,* PhD diss., Ruprecht-Karls-Universität Heidelberg, 1974.

Albstadt 2005
Christian Landenberger: Blickpunkte, exh. cat., Galerie Albstadt, 2005.

Albstadt 2012
Christian Landenberger 1862–1927—Adolf Luther 1912–1990; Spiegelbilder/Lichtreflexe, exh. cat., Galerie Albstadt, 2012.

Alkersum 2016
Max Liebermann und Zeitgenossen: Neue Werke in der Sammlung, exh. cat., Museum Kunst der Westküste, Alkersum/Föhr 2016.

Avenarius 1907
Ferdinand Avenarius, *Liebermann-Mappe,* Munich [1907].

Baden-Baden 1985
Deutsche Impressionisten aus dem Niedersächsischen Landesmuseum Hannover, exh. cat., Staatliche Kunsthalle Baden-Baden, 1985.

Baden-Baden 2014
Lesser Ury und das Licht, exh. cat., Museum für Kunst und Technik des 19. Jahrhunderts, Baden-Baden 2014.

Balzer 1948
Wolfgang Balzer, *Max Liebermann: 12 Zeichnungen,* Dresden 1948.

Bappert et al. 1992
Theseus Bappert et al., *Ein Wannsee-Bilderbuch,* Berlin 1992.

Berend-Corinth 1958
Charlotte Berend-Corinth, *Mein Leben mit Lovis Corinth,* Munich 1958.

Berlin 1911
Katalog der XXII. Ausstellung der Berliner Secession, exh. cat., Ausstellungshaus am Kurfürstendamm, Berlin 1911.

Berlin 1928
*Max Slevogt: Gemälde, Aquarelle, Pastelle, Zeichnungen zu seinem 60. Geburtstag*e, exh. cat., Preußische Akademie der Künste, Berlin 1928.

Berlin 1931
Lesser Ury: Gedenkausstellung, exh. cat., Nationalgalerie, Berlin 1931.

Berlin 1947
Gedächtnisausstellung: Max Liebermann zum 100. Geburtstag, exh. cat., Magistrat von Groß-Berlin, Hauptamt für Kunst, Ausstellungsräume des Westens, Berlin 1947.

Berlin 1961
Lesser Ury: Ausstellung anlässlich des 100. Geburtstages, exh. cat., Galerie am Lützowplatz/Bezirksamt Tiergarten, Berlin 1961.

Berlin 1970
Der Berliner Maler Franz Skarbina: Ein Querschnitt durch sein Werk, exh. cat., Große Galerie des Berlin-Museums, 1970.

Berlin 1979
Max Liebermann in seiner Zeit, exh. cat., Nationalgalerie, Berlin 1979.

Berlin 1981
Maria Slavona, 1865–1931: Eine deutsche Impressionistin, exh. cat., Sammlung Bröhan, Berlin 1981.

Berlin 1985
Für Max Liebermann, 1847–1935, exh. cat., Nationalgalerie, Berlin 1985.

Berlin 1995a
Franz Skarbina, exh. cat., Bröhan-Museum, Berlin 1995.

Berlin 1995b
Lesser Ury: Zauber des Lichts, exh. cat., Käthe-Kollwitz-Museum, Berlin 1995.

Berlin 1997a
Max Liebermann: Jahrhundertwende, exh. cat., Nationalgalerie, Berlin 1997.

Berlin 1997b
Max Liebermann: Was vom Leben übrig bleibt, sind Bilder und Geschichten; Max Liebermann zum 150. Geburtstag; Rekonstruktion der Gedächtnisausstellung des Berliner Jüdischen Museums von 1936, exh. cat., Stiftung Neue Synagoge Berlin—Centrum Judaicum Berlin, 1997.

Berlin 2001
Im Streit um die Moderne: Max Liebermann, der Kaiser, die Nationalgalerie Berlin, exh. cat., Nationalgalerie, Berlin 2001.

Berlin 2007
Martha Liebermann: Lebensbilder, exh. cat., Liebermann-Villa am Wannsee, Berlin 2007.

Berlin 2008
Max Liebermann: Der Birkenweg; Ein Motiv zwischen Impressionismus und Jugendstil, exh. cat., Liebermann-Villa am Wannsee, Berlin 2008.

Berlin 2009a
Der Jesus-Skandal: Ein Liebermann-Bild im Kreuzfeuer der Kritik, exh. cat., Liebermann-Villa am Wannsee, Berlin 2009.

Berlin 2009b
Die Papageienallee am Wannsee: Die Liebermann-Sammlung der Kunsthalle Bremen zu Gast, exh. cat., Liebermann-Villa am Wannsee, Berlin 2009.

Berlin 2009c
Künstlerfürsten: Max Liebermann, Franz von Lenbach, Franz von Stuck, exh. cat., Stiftung Brandenburger Tor, Berlin 2009.

Berlin 2010a
Die Idee vom Haus im Grünen: Max Liebermann am Wannsee, exh. cat., Liebermann-Villa am Wannsee, Berlin 2010.

Berlin 2010b
Ein öffentlicher Kopf: Max Liebermann in Bildnissen, Fotografien und Karikaturen, exh. cat., Liebermann-Villa am Wannsee, Berlin 2010.

Berlin 2011
Max Liebermann am Meer, exh. cat., Liebermann-Villa am Wannsee, Berlin 2011.

Berlin 2013
Max Liebermann und Frankreich, exh. cat., Liebermann-Villa am Wannsee, Berlin 2013.

Berlin 2016
Max Liebermann—Biergärten und Caféterrassen: Von ländlicher Wirtschaft zu bürgerlicher Sommerfrische, exh. cat., Liebermann-Villa am Wannsee, Berlin 2016.

Berlin 2019a
Kampf um Sichtbarkeit: Künstlerinnen der Nationalgalerie vor 1919, exh. cat., Nationalgalerie, Berlin 2019.

Berlin 2019b
Max Liebermann und Lesser Ury: Zweimal Großstadt Berlin, exh. cat., Liebermann-Villa am Wannsee, Berlin 2019.

Berlin 2019c
Sehnsucht nach Idylle: Max Liebermann und die Maler am Wannsee, exh. cat., Liebermann-Villa am Wannsee, Berlin 2019.

Berlin 2024a
Dora Hitz: Mit dem Alten um das Neue kämpfen, exh. cat., Liebermann Villa am Wannsee, Berlin 2024.

Berlin 2024b
Monet and the Impressionist Cityscape, exh. cat., Nationalgalerie, Berlin 2024.

Bertuleit 1994
Sigrid Bertuleit, *Max Liebermann: Gemälde 1873–1918,* Hannover 1994.

Bertuleit 2001
Sigrid Bertuleit, *Der Garten des Künstlers: Zum Gemälde "Die Blumenterrasse im Wannseegarten nach Nordwesten," wohl 1924,* Schweinfurt 2001.

Bertuleit 2007
Sigrid Bertuleit, *Flora: Blumenstücke und Stillleben von Lovis Corinth,* Schweinfurt 2007.

Bie 1911
Oscar Bie, *Max Liebermann: Holländisches Skizzenbuch,* Berlin 1911.

Bielefeld 2009
Der deutsche Impressionismus, exh. cat., Kunsthalle Bielefeld, 2009.

Bietigheim-Bissingen 2001
Kinderblicke: Kindheit und Moderne von Klee bis Boltanski, exh. cat., Städtische Galerie Bietigheim-Bissingen, 2001.

Bonn 2011
Max Liebermann: Wegbereiter der Moderne, exh. cat., Kunst und Ausstellungshalle der Bundesrepublik Deutschland, Bonn 2011.

Boskamp 1994
Katrin Boskamp, *Studien zum Frühwerk von Max Liebermann mit einem Verzeichnis der Gemälde und Ölstudien von 1866–1889,* Studien zur Kunstgeschichte 88, Hildesheim 1994.

Braun/Braun 2008
Max Liebermanns Garten am Wannsee, ed. Günter Braun and Waldtraud Braun, Berlin 2008.

Brauner 1986
Lothar Brauner, *Max Liebermann,* Berlin 1986.

Braunschweig 2008
Max Liebermann in Braunschweig, exh. cat., Galerie Städtisches Museum und Sammlung Bönsch, Braunschweig 2008.

Bremen 1995
"Nichts trügt weniger als der Schein": Max Liebermann—der deutsche Impressionist, exh. cat., Kunsthalle Bremen, 1995.

Bremen 1998
Fritz von Uhde: Vom Realismus zum Impressionismus; Eine Wiederentdeckung, exh. cat., Kunsthalle Bremen, 1998.

Bremen 2016
Max Liebermann: Vom Freizeitvergnügen zum modernen Sport, exh. cat., Kunsthalle Bremen, 2016.

Breslau 1937
Konrad von Kardorff: Ausstellung ausgewählter Bilder anlässlich seines 60. Geburtstages, exh. cat., Schlesisches Museum der Bildenden Künste, Breslau 1937.

Brieger-Wasservogel 1906
Lothar Brieger-Wasservogel, *Der Fall Liebermann: Über Virtuosentum in der bildenden Kunst,* Stuttgart 1906.

Bröhan 2022
Nicole Bröhan, *Max Liebermann: Eine Biographie,* Berlin 2022.

Bunge 1990
Matthias Bunge, *Max Liebermann als Künstler der Farbe,* Berlin 1990.

Burr 1910
Wilhelm F. Burr, *Max Liebermann: Eine Kunstgabe von 14 Bildern,* Mainz 1910.

Busch 1986
Günter Busch, *Max Liebermann, Maler—Zeichner—Graphiker,* Frankfurt am Main 1986.

Cassirer/Cassirer 1898
Mappe mit 6 Kaltnadelradierungen Max Liebermanns, ed. Bruno and Paul Cassirer, Berlin 1898.

Chatou 2014
L'Enfant vu par les peintres au 19e siècle, exh. cat., Musée Fournaise, Chatou 2014.

Chemnitz 2011
Max Slevogt: Malerei und Grafik, exh. cat., Kunstsammlungen Chemnitz, 2011.

Cologne 2010
German Impressionist Landscape Painting: Liebermann—Corinth—Slevogt, exh. cat., Wallraf-Richartz-Museum & Fondation Corboud, Cologne 2010.

Cologne 2024
Paris 1863 • 1874—Revolution in der Kunst: Vom Salon zum Impressionismus, exh. cat., Wallraf-Richartz-Museum & Fondation Corboud, Cologne 2024.

Corinth 1926
Lovis Corinth, *Selbstbiographie,* Leipzig 1926.

Corinth 1979
Thomas Corinth, *Lovis Corinth: Eine Dokumentation,* Tübingen 1979.

Deshmukh 2011
Max Liebermann and International Modernism: An Artist's Career from Empire to Third Reich, ed. Marion Deshmukh, New York 2011.

Deshmukh 2015
Marion Deshmukh, *Max Liebermann: Modern Art and Modern Germany*, Farnham 2015.

Dorgeloh 2003
Annette Dorgerloh, *Das Künstlerehepaar Lepsius: Zur Berliner Porträtmalerei um 1900,* Berlin 2003.

Dortmund 2020
Emil Nolde, Christian Rohlfs, exh. cat., Galerie Utermann, Dortmund 2020.

Dresden 1993
Gotthardt Kuehl, 1850–1915, exh. cat., Staatliche Kunstsammlungen Dresden, Gemäldegalerie Neue Meister, 1993.

Dresden 2008
Max Liebermann in der Dresdener Galerie, coll. cat., Staatliche Kunstsammlungen Dresden, Galerie Neue Meister, 2008.

Dresden 2012
Max Slevogt in der Dresdener Galerie, exh. cat., Staatliche Kunstsammlungen Dresden, Gemäldegalerie Neue Meister, 2012.

Dresden 2014
Max Slevogt: Die Reise nach Ägypten 1914, exh. cat., Staatliche Kunstsammlungen Dresden, Galerie Neue Meister, 2014.

Eberle 1995–96
Matthias Eberle, *Max Liebermann, 1847–1935: Werkverzeichnis der Gemälde und Ölstudien,* vol. 1: *1865–1899,* Munich 1995, vol. 2: *1900–1935,* Munich 1996.

Eckert 1994
Reinald Eckert, *Garten Max Liebermann: Berlin-Wannsee; Eine gartenhistorische Untersuchung zu Geschichte, Bestand und zukünftigem Umgang mit dem Grundstück am Großen Wannsee 42 in Berlin-Wannsee,* 2 vols., Berlin 1994.

Edenkoben 1991a
Max Slevogt: Die Zauberflöte; Randzeichnungen zu Mozarts Handschrift, exh. cat., Max-Slevogt-Galerie Schloss Villa Ludwigshöhe, Edenkoben 1991.

Edenkoben 1991b
Slevogt und Mozart: Werke von Max Slevogt zu den Opern "Don Giovanni" und "Die Zauberflöte," exh. cat., Max-Slevogt-Galerie Schloss Villa Ludwigshöhe, Edenkoben 1991.

Edenkoben 2007
Tänzerinnen um Slevogt, exh. cat., Max-Slevogt-Galerie Schloss Villa Ludwigshöhe, Edenkoben 2007.

Edenkoben 2009
Max Slevogt in der Pfalz, coll. cat., Max-Slevogt-Galerie Schloss Villa Ludwigshöhe, 2nd ed., Edenkoben 2009.

Edenkoben 2019
Lesser Ury: Der Einzelgänger unter den "Deutschen Impressionisten," exh. cat., Max-Slevogt-Galerie Schloss Villa Ludwigshöhe, Edenkoben 2019.

Eder 1991
Irene Eder, *Friedrich Kallmorgen, 1856–1924: Monographie und Werkverzeichnis der Gemälde und Druckgraphik,* Karlsruhe 1991.

Eipper 1971
Paul Eipper, *Ateliergespräche mit Liebermann und Corinth,* Munich 1971.

Englert 1995
Lovis Corinth, *Gesammelte Schriften,* ed. Kerstin Englert, Berlin 1995.

Erlangen 1980
Charlotte Berend-Corinth: Eine Ausstellung zum 100. Geburtstag der Künstlerin, exh. cat., Kunstverein Erlangen, 1980.

Essen 2010
Bilder einer Metropole: Die Impressionisten in Paris, exh. cat., Museum Folkwang, Essen 2010.

Feist 1993
Impressionismus: Die Entdeckung der Freizeit, ed. Peter H. Feist, Leipzig 1993.

Frankfurt am Main 2001
Wilhelm Trübner: Die Frankfurter Jahre, 1896–1903; Ausstellung anläßlich seines 150. Geburtstages, Haus Giersch—Museum Regionaler Kunst, Frankfurt am Main 2001.

Frankfurt am Main 2006
Die Eroberung der Straße: Von Monet bis Grosz, exh. cat., Schirn Kunsthalle Frankfurt [am Main], 2006.

Frankfurt am Main 2010
Der Maler Philipp Franck (1860–1944): Vom Taunus zum Wannsee, exh. cat., Museum Giersch, Frankfurt am Main 2010.

Fuß 2013
Rowena Fuß, *Christian Rohlfs in Weimar: Das Frühwerk 1870 bis 1901,* Weimar 2013.

Geißler 1973
Joachim Geißler, *Die Kunsttheorien von A. Hildebrandt, W. Trübner und Max Liebermann: Ein Beitrag zur Geschichte der Kunstliteratur in Deutschland,* PhD diss. Ruprecht-Karls-Universität Heidelberg, 1973.

Görgen/Giesen 2002
Annabelle Görgen and Sebastian Giesen, *Ein Impressionismus für Hamburgs Bürgertum: Max Liebermann und Alfred Lichtwark,* Hamburg 2002.

Gutgesell 2019
Natalie Gutgesell, *Dora Hitz: Fränkische Künstlerin, rumänische Hofmalerin, europäische Avantgardistin,* Halle an der Saale 2019.

Guthmann 1917
Johannes Guthmann, *Bilder aus Ägypten: Aquarelle und Zeichnungen von Max Slevogt,* Berlin 1917.

Guthmann 1920
Johannes Guthmann, *Scherz und Laune: Max Slevogt und seine Gelegenheitsarbeiten,* Berlin 1920.

Hagen 2009
Christian Rohlfs, Musik der Farben, coll. cat., Osthaus Museum Hagen, 2009.

Halle an der Saale 2000
Kindsein ist kein Kinderspiel: Das Jahrhundert des Kindes (1900–1999), exh. cat., Franckesche Stiftungen zu Halle, 2000.

Hamburg 1994
Max Liebermann in Hamburg: Landschaften zwischen Alster und Elbe 1890–1910, exh. cat., Hamburger Kunsthalle, 1994.

Hamburg 1997
Max Liebermann: Der Realist und die Phantasie, exh. cat., Hamburger Kunsthalle, 1997.

Hamburg 2004
Im Garten von Max Liebermann, exh. cat., Hamburger Kunsthalle, 2004.

Hamburg 2021
Impressionismus—deutsch-französische Begegnungen, exh. cat., Hamburger Kunsthalle, 2021.

Hancke 1914
Erich Hancke, *Max Liebermann: Sein Leben und seine Werke,* Berlin 1914.

The Hague 1980
Max Liebermann en Holland, exh. cat., Haags Gemeentemuseum, The Hague 1980.

The Hague 2018
Max Liebermann: Een zomers impressionist, exh. cat., Gemeentemuseum Den Haag, The Hague 2018.

Hannover 1954
Max Liebermann, 1847–1935, exh. cat., Niedersächsisches Landesmuseum Hannover, 1954.

Hannover 1965
Max Slevogt: Graphik und Handzeichnungen, exh. cat., Kestner-Museum Hannover, 1965.

Hannover 1994
Max Liebermann und Barbizon: Landleben—Naturerlebnis, exh. cat., Niedersächsisches Landesmuseum Hannover, 1994.

Hannover 1997
Corinth, Liebermann, Slevogt: Die Zeichnungen der Niedersächsischen Landesgalerie, coll. cat., Forum des Landesmuseums Hannover, 1997.

Hannover 1999
Max Slevogt: Gemälde 1889–1931, coll. cat., Niedersächsisches Landesmuseum Hannover, 1999.

Hannover 2006
Max Liebermann und die Holländer, exh. cat., Niedersächsisches Landesmuseum Hannover, 2006.

Hannover 2017
Nackt und bloß: Lovis Corinth und der Akt um 1900, exh. cat., Niedersächsisches Landesmuseum Hannover, 2017.

Hannover 2018
Max Slevogt: Eine Retrospektive zum 150. Geburtstag, exh. cat., Niedersächsisches Landesmuseum Hannover, 2018

Hannover 2021
Im Freien: Von Monet bis Corinth, exh. cat., Niedersächsisches Landesmuseum Hannover, 2021.

Hedinger et al. 2013
Max Liebermann: Die Kunstsammlung; Von Rembrandt bis Manet, ed. Bärbel Hedinger et al., Munich 2013.

Heidelberg 1994
Wilhelm Trübner, 1851–1917, exh. cat., Kurpfälzisches Museum, Heidelberg 1994.

Heikendorf 2005
Schleswig-Holstein bildumschlungen: Georg Burmester und die Schleswig-Holsteinische Kunstgenossenschaft, exh. cat., Künstlermuseum Heikendorf—Kieler Förde, 2005.

Höfchen 1986
Heinz Höfchen, *Christian Landenberger,* ed. Alfred Hagenlocher, Stuttgart 1986.

Hoke 2011
Sarah Hoke, *Fritz von Uhdes "Kinderstube": Die Darstellung des Kindes in seinem Spiel- und Wohnmilieu,* Göttingen 2011.

Imiela 1962
Hans-Jürgen Imiela, *Max Slevogt: Das druckgraphische Werk,* vol. 1: *Radierungen, Lithographien, Holzschnitte, 1890–1914,* Heidelberg 1962.

Imiela 1968
Hans-Jürgen Imiela, *Max Slevogt: Eine Monographie,* Karlsruhe 1968.

Immenhausen/von Tresckow 2010
Wolfgang Immenhausen and Almut von Tresckow, *Philipp Franck (1860–1944): Werkverzeichnis der Gemälde,* Berlin 2010.

Innsbruck 2003
In freier Natur: Von Cézanne bis Picasso; Mensch und Landschaft in der europäischen Moderne, exh. cat., Tiroler Landesmuseum Ferdinandeum, Innsbruck 2003.

Kaiserslautern 1966
Max Slevogt: Religiöse Werke; Gemälde, Aquarelle, Graphiken 1887–1932, exh. cat., Pfalzgalerie Kaiserslautern, 1966.

Karlsruhe 1991
Mit Kallmorgen unterwegs: Zeichnungen und Gemälde von 1880 bis 1920, exh. cat., Städtische Galerie im Prinz-Max-Palais, Karlsruhe 1991.

Karlsruhe 2016
Kallmorgen: Malerei zwischen Realismus und Impressionismus, exh. cat., Staatliche Kunsthalle Karlsruhe, 2016.

Kern 1989
Josef Kern, *Impressionismus im Wilhelminischen Deutschland: Studien zur Kunst- und Kulturgeschichte des Kaiserreichs*, PhD diss., Universität Würzburg, 1989.

Kiel 2012
Überwältigend kühn: Der ganze Rohlfs in Kiel, exh. cat., Kunsthalle zu Kiel, 2012.

Kitchen/Drost 2007
Deutsche Kunst: Französische Perspektiven 1870–1945; Quellen und Kommentare zur Kunstkritik, ed. Friederike Kitchen and Julia Drost, Berlin 2007.

Kochel am See 2009
Lovis Corinth: Seelenlandschaften; Walchenseebilder und Selbstbildnisse, exh. cat., Franz Marc Museum, Kochel am See 2009.

Konstanz 2020
Malerei süddeutscher Impressionisten: Licht, Luft und Farbe, exh. cat., Städtische Wessenberg-Galerie, Konstanz 2020.

Kropmanns 2008
Peter Kropmanns, *Lovis Corinth: Ein Künstlerleben,* Stuttgart 2008.

Küster 1988
Bernd Küster, *Max Liebermann: Ein Malerleben,* Hamburg 1988.

Landshut 2009
Mit Phantasie und Schöpferlaune: Max Slevogt als Graphiker und Illustrator, exh. cat., Museen der Stadt Landshut, 2009.

Lata 2023
Sabine Lata, *Lesser Ury: Maler der Moderne,* Berlin 2023.

Leipzig 2008
Lovis Corinth und die Geburt der Moderne, exh. cat., Museum der bildenden Künste, Leipzig 2008.

Leipzig 2019
Impressionismus in Leipzig 1900–1914: Liebermann, Slevogt, Corinth, exh. cat., Museum der bildenden Künste Leipzig, 2019.

Liebermann 1922
Max Liebermann, *Gesammelte Schriften,* Berlin 1922.

Liebermann 1978
Max Liebermann, *Die Phantasie in der Malerei: Schriften und Reden,* ed. Günter Busch, Frankfurt am Main 1978.

Liebermann 1993
Max Liebermann, *Vision der Wirklichkeit: Ausgewählte Schriften und Reden,* ed. Günter Busch, Frankfurt am Main 1993.

Liebermann 2011
Max Liebermann, *Briefe,* ed. Ernst Braun, vol. 1: *1869–1895,* Baden-Baden 2011.

Liebermann 2012
Max Liebermann, *Briefe,* ed. Ernst Braun, vol. 2: *1896–1901,* Baden-Baden 2012.

Liebermann 2013
Max Liebermann, *Briefe,* ed. Ernst Braun, vol. 3: *1902–1906,* Baden-Baden 2013.

Liebermann 2014
Max Liebermann, *Briefe,* ed. Ernst Braun, vol. 4: *1907–1910,* Baden-Baden 2014.

Liebermann 2015
Max Liebermann, *Briefe,* ed. Ernst Braun, vol. 5: *1911–1915,* Baden-Baden 2015.

Liebermann 2016
Max Liebermann, *Briefe,* ed. Ernst Braun, vol. 6: *1916–1921,* Baden-Baden 2016.

Liebermann 2017
Max Liebermann, *Briefe,* ed. Ernst Braun, vol. 7: *1922–1926,* Baden-Baden 2017.

Liebermann 2019
Max Liebermann, *Briefe,* ed. Ernst Braun, vol. 8: *1927–1935,* Baden-Baden 2019.

Liebermann 2021a
Max Liebermann, *Briefe,* ed. Ernst Braun, vol. 9,1: *Nachträge,* Baden-Baden 2021.

Liebermann 2021b
Max Liebermann, *Briefe,* ed. Ernst Braun, vol. 9,2: *Nachträge: Die Ausstellungen der Werke Max Liebermanns zwischen 1870 und 1945,* Baden-Baden 2021.

Limbach-Oberfrohna 2011
Die Göttlichkeit des Lichts: Fritz von Uhde (1848–1911) zum 100. Todestag, exh. cat., Schloss Wolkenburg, Limbach-Oberfrohna 2011.

Los Angeles 2005
Max Liebermann: From Realism to Impressionism, exh. cat., Skirball Cultural Center, Los Angeles 2005.

Ludewig 2012
Aufbruch in die Moderne: Sammler, Mäzene und Kunsthändler in Berlin 1880–1933, ed. Anna-Dorothea Ludewig, Cologne 2012.

Mainz 1989
Max Slevogt: Ägyptenreise 1914, exh. cat., Landesmuseum Mainz, 1989.

Mainz 2013
Max Slevogt: Neue Wege des Impressionismus, exh. cat., Landesmuseum Mainz, 2013.

Mainz 2018
Ein Tag am Meer: Slevogt, Liebermann & Cassirer, exh. cat., Landesmuseum Mainz, 2018.

Meier-Graefe 1904
Julius Meier-Graefe, *Entwicklungsgeschichte der modernen Kunst: Vergleichende Betrachtung der bildenden Künste, als Beitrag zu einer neuen Aesthetik,* 3 vols., Stuttgart 1904.

Mommsen 1994
Wolfgang Mommsen, *Bürgerliche Kultur und künstlerische Avantgarde 1870–1918: Kultur und Politik im deutschen Kaiserreich,* Munich 1994.

Munich 1996a
Christian Rohlfs: 1849–1938, exh. cat., Kunsthalle der Hypo-Kulturstiftung München, Munich 1996.

Munich 1996b
Lovis Corinth: Retrospektive, exh. cat., Haus der Kunst, Munich 1996.

Nedelykov/Moreira 2003
Nina Nedelykov and Pedro Moreira, *Zurück am Wannsee: Max Liebermanns Sommerhaus,* Berlin 2003.

Nedelykov/Moreira 2006
Nina Nedelykov and Pedro Moreira, *Max Liebermann: Das Paradies am Wannsee,* Berlin 2006.

Neu-Ulm 2015
Die Malweiber von Paris: Deutsche Künstlerinnen im Aufbruch, exh. cat., Edwin Scharff Museum, Neu-Ulm 2015.

Owesle 2016
Miriam-Esther Owesle, *Franz Skarbina 1849–1910: Natur und Pose; Ein Künstler zwischen Realismus und Poesie,* Hamburg 2016.

Palmbach 2001
Barbara Palmbach, *Paris und der Impressionismus: Die Großstadt als Impuls für neue Wahrnehmungsformen und Ausdrucksmöglichkeiten in der Malerei,* Weimar 2001.

Passarge 1961
Walter Passarge, *Slevogt: Wand- und Deckengemälde auf Neukastel,* Berlin 1961.

Pflugmacher 2003
Der Briefwechsel zwischen Alfred Lichtwark und Max Liebermann, ed. Birgit Pflugmacher, Hildesheim 2003.

Pforzheim 2005
Charlotte Berend-Corinth, Lovis Corinth: Ein Künstlerpaar im Berlin der Klassischen Moderne, exh. cat., Reuchlinhaus Pforzheim, 2005.

Regensburg 1986
Lovis Corinth, die Bilder vom Walchensee: Vision und Realität, exh. cat., Ostdeutsche Galerie, Regensburg, 1986.

Rendsburg 2003
Max Liebermann 1847–1935: "Ich bin doch nur ein Maler," exh. cat., Jüdisches Museum Rendsburg, Stiftung Schleswig-Holsteinische Landesmuseen Schloss Gottorf, Rendsburg 2003.

Roland 1991
Berthold Roland, *Max Slevogt: Pfälzische Landschaften,* Munich 1991.

Saarbrücken 1992
Max Slevogt: Gemälde, Aquarelle, Zeichnungen, exh. cat., Saarland Museum, Saarbrücken 1992.

Saarbrücken 2006
Slevogt und Mozart: Illustrationen zu den Opern "Don Giovanni" und "Die Zauberflöte," Saarlandmuseum, Saarbrücken 2006.

Saarbrücken 2018
Slevogt und Frankreich, exh. cat., Saarland-museum, Saarbrücken 2018.

Saarbrücken 2021
Charlotte Berend-Corinth: Wiederentdeckt!, exh. cat., Saarlandmuseum, Saarbrücken 2021.

Salzburg 1996
Mozarts Opern im Werk von Max Slevogt und Hans Meid, exh. cat., Internationale Stiftung Mozarteum, Salzburg 1996.

Sandig 2005
Marina Sandig, *Die Liebermanns: Ein biographisches Zeit- und Kulturbild der preußisch-jüdischen Familie und Verwandtschaft von Max Liebermann,* Neustadt an der Aisch 2005.

Scheer 2006
Regina Scheer, *"Wir sind die Liebermanns": Die Geschichte einer Familie,* Berlin 2006.

Scheer 2010
Regina Scheer, *Max Liebermann erzählt aus seinem Leben,* Berlin 2010.

Scheidig 1991
Walther Scheidig, *Die Weimarer Malerschule: 1860–1900,* Leipzig 1991.

Schellenberg 1947
Alfred Lichtwark: Briefe an Max Liebermann, ed. Carl Schellenberg, Hamburg 1947.

Schenk 2015
Carola Schenk, *Die Bühnenbildentwürfe im Werk von Max Slevogt,* PhD diss., Ludwig-Maximilians-Universität München, Munich 2015.

Schlör 1994
Joachim Schlör, *Nachts in der großen Stadt: Paris, Berlin, London, 1840–1930,* Munich 1994.

Schmalhausen 1994
Bernd Schmalhausen, *"Ich bin doch nur ein Maler": Max und Martha Liebermann im "Dritten Reich,"* Hildesheim 1994.

Schmidt 2019
Sophie Schmidt, *Dora Hitz: Was sie als Künstlerin prägte und wodurch sich ihre Kunst auszeichnet,* Munich 2019.

Schrohe 2024
Rahel Schrohe, *Dora Hitz: Wechselspiele von Weiblichkeit und Raum,* Berlin 2024.

Schwäbisch Hall 2003
Max Liebermann: Poesie des einfachen Lebens, exh. cat., Kunsthalle Würth, Schwäbisch Hall 2003.

Schweinfurt 2001
Max Liebermann: Die Frau im Hintergrund, exh. cat., Museum Georg Schäfer, Schweinfurt 2001.

Schweinfurt 2022
Les Amusements: Max Slevogts Inspirationen durch Bühne und Literatur, exh. cat., Museum Georg Schäfer, Schweinfurt 2022.

Seyppel 1987
Joachim Seyppel, *Lesser Ury: Der Maler der alten City; Leben—Kunst—Wirkung; eine Monographie,* Berlin 1987.

Stuttgart 1986
Christian Landenberger: Gemälde, Zeichnungen und Radierungen, coll. cat., Galerie der Stadt Stuttgart, 1986.

Teut 1997
Anna Teut, *Max Liebermann: Gartenparadies am Wannsee,* Munich 1997.

Thomas 2010
Greg M. Thomas, *Impressionist Children: Childhood, Family, and Modern Identity in French Art,* New Haven 2010.

Vienna 1992
Lovis Corinth, exh. cat., Bank Austria Kunstforum, Vienna 1992.

Vienna 1997
Max Liebermann und die französischen Impressionisten, exh. cat., Jüdisches Museum der Stadt Wien, Vienna 1997.

Vienna 2009
Lovis Corinth: Ein Fest der Malerei, exh. cat., Belvedere, Vienna 2009.

Vienna 2021
Lovis Corinth: Das Leben, ein Fest!, exh. cat., Belvedere, Vienna 2021.

Von Brauchitsch 2013
Boris von Brauchitsch, *Lesser Ury: Leichte Fieberanfälle; Dauerregen,* Berlin 2013.

Wadersloh 2019
Inspiration Licht: Impressionisten aus dem Süden zu Gast bei Max Liebermann, exh. cat., Museum Abtei Liesborn, Wadersloh 2019.

Warzecha 2022
Jasper Warzecha, *Gotthardt Kuehl und der "Figürliche Impressionismus,"* Berlin 2022.

Wedekind 2016
Blick zurück nach vorn: Neue Forschungen zu Max Slevogt, ed. Gregor Wedekind, Göttingen 2016.

Wedekind 2021
Max Slevogts Netzwerke: Kunst-, Kultur- und Intellektuellengeschichte des späten Kaiserreichs und der Weimarer Republik, ed. Gregor Wedekind, Berlin 2021.

Weimar 1999
Aufstieg und Fall der Moderne: Weimar—ein deutsches Beispiel 1890–1990, exh. cat., Kunstsammlungen zu Weimar 1999.

Weimar 2010
Hinaus in die Natur! Barbizon, die Weimarer Malerschule und der Aufbruch zum Impressionismus, exh. cat., Neues Museum Weimar, 2010.

Weimar 2021
Landschaften im Licht: Der Impressionist Ludwig von Gleichen-Rußwurm, exh. cat., Klassik Stiftung Weimar, 2021.

Wertheim 2008
Max Liebermann und norddeutsche Künstler der Berliner Secession, exh. cat., Museum Schlösschen im Hofgarten, Wertheim 2008.

Wilhelmshaven 1998
Malerfreunde: Max Slevogt und Robert Breyer, exh. cat., Kunsthalle Wilhelmshaven 1998.

Wuppertal 2005a
Hans Thoma, Max Liebermann, Max Slevogt: Aus der Graphischen Sammlung des Von der Heydt-Museums Wuppertal, exh. cat., Von der Heydt-Museum, Wuppertal 2005.

Wuppertal 2005b
Max Slevogt: Die Berliner Jahre, exh. cat., Von der Heydt-Museum, Wuppertal 2005.

Würzburg 1983
Ludwig von Gleichen-Rußwurm, exh. cat., Städtische Galerie Würzburg, 1983.

Ziegler 2001
Hendrik Ziegler, *Die Kunst der Weimarer Malerschule: Von der Pleinairmalerei zum Impressionismus,* Cologne 2001.

Authors

Alexander Bastek, director of the Museum Behnhaus Drägerhaus in Lübeck since 2008, studied art history, history, and philosophy in Bochum and Pisa as well as in Hamburg, where he received his doctorate in 2005 with the dissertation "Ferdinand Brütt und das städtisch-bürgerliche Genre um 1900." He worked as an intern and then a research associate at the Museum Giersch in Frankfurt am Main; his publications and exhibitions on nineteenth- and early twentieth-century art include *Carl Friedrich von Rumohr* (2011), *Anders Zorn* (2012), *Thomas Mann und die bildende Kunst* (2014), and *Irr-Real: Carl Julius Milde, das Porträt und die Psychiatrie*. Since 2010 he has taught courses in the art history department of the Universität Hamburg. He is a member of the board of trustees of the Hans-Meid-Stiftung (book illustration), the advisory board of the Overbeck-Gesellschaft, and the board of directors of the Verein für Lübeckische Geschichte und Altertumskunde.

Karoline Feulner, head of the department of painting and sculpture at the Landesmuseum Mainz since 2013 and head of research at the Max-Slevogt-Galerie at Schloss Villa Ludwigshöhe in Edenkoben since 2015, received her doctorate from the Johannes Gutenberg-Universität in Mainz with a dissertation on the reception of Albrecht Dürer in the twentieth century (2010). She has served as a research associate at the Universität Mainz and as an intern and then research associate at the Städel Museum in Frankfurt am Main, where she worked on the exhibitions *Beckmann & Amerika* (2011) and *Dürer: Kunst—Künstler—Kontext* (2013). She has curated numerous exhibitions at the Landesmuseum Mainz, including *Ein Stück norddeutscher Himmel: Emil Nolde und die Künstler der "Brücke"* (2016), *Ein Tag am Meer: Slevogt, Liebermann & Cassirer* (2018), *Hexenküche: Max Slevogts druckgrafische Experimente* (2021), *Blauer Aufbruch: Malerei der Quadriga nach 1945* (2023), and currently *"Auf zu neuen Werken!": Max Slevogt und sein Verleger Bruno Cassirer* (2025).

Valentina Plotnikova, assistant curator at the Museum Barberini in Potsdam since 2024, was a curatorial assistant at the Galerie für zeitgenössische Kunst Bode in Berlin from 2020 to 2024. She studied art history at the Humboldt-Universität zu Berlin and completed her master's thesis on artificial light as a protagonist in Lesser Ury's nocturnal urban landscape paintings in 2024. From 2015 to 2019 she worked in the area of international public relations after studying international relations at the Freie Universität Berlin and the Moscow State Institute of International Relations from 2009 to 2015 with the master's thesis "Soft Power Index: Germany and Russia" (2015). She contributed to the exhibition catalogs *Maurice de Vlaminck: Modern Art Rebel* (2024) and *Unicorn: The Mythical Beast in Art* (2025) and served as curatorial assistant for the exhibitions *The Honest Eye: Camille Pissarro's Impressionism* (2025) and *Unicorn: The Mythical Beast in Art* (2025), as well as assisting with preparations for *Symphonies of Color: Signac and Neo-Impressionism* (2026).

Christiane Righetti, research associate at the Museum Frieder Burda in Baden-Baden since 2008, previously worked in a gallery for contemporary art in London and completed a two-year training position at the Kunstsammlungen und Museen Augsburg (Museum für Gegenwartskunst) and internships at the Museum of Modern Art in New York and the Neue Nationalgalerie in Berlin. She studied art history at the Università degli Studi di Firenze and Aarhus Universitet, receiving a laurea degree in 2004. She has participated in over thirty exhibition projects including *Fabrizio Plessi: Lava* (2006) at the Museum für Gegenwartskunst in Augsburg as well as *Der Blaue Reiter* (2009), *Miró: Die Farben der Poesie* (2010), *Léger—Laurens: Tête-à-Tête* (2012), *Franz Gertsch* (2013), *Heinz Mack* (2015), *Die Kerze* (2016), *Die Brücke* (2018), *Ensemble* (2019), *Soulages* (2020), and *Yoshitomo Nara* (2024) at the Museum Frieder Burda in Baden-Baden.

Barbara Schaefer, deputy director of the Wallraf-Richartz-Museum & Fondation Corboud in Cologne since 2013, has worked there since 1999 and has been head of the department of eighteenth- and nineteenth-century painting and sculpture since 2012. She has curated special exhibitions including *Künstlerpaare: Liebe, Kunst und Leidenschaft* (2008–09), *1912—Mission Moderne: Die Jahrhundertschau des Sonderbundes* (2012), *Von Dürer bis van Gogh: Sammlung Bührle trifft Wallraf* (2016–17), *Es war einmal in Amerika: 300 Jahre US-amerikanische Kunst* (2018–19, cocurated with Anita Hachmann), *Paris 1863 • 1874: Revolution in der Kunst—Vom Salon zum Impressionismus* (2024), and *Schweizer Schätze: Meisterwerke des Impressionismus aus dem Museum Langmatt* (2025).

Lucy Wasensteiner, junior professor of art-historical provenance research at the Universität Bonn since 2024, completed her doctorate at the Courtauld Institute of Art in London with a dissertation on the 1938 London exhibition *Twentieth Century German Art,* the largest international response to the Nazi "Degenerate Art" campaign. Subsequently she worked as a researcher and writer for the Tate Gallery, as an associate lecturer at the Courtauld Institute, and from 2018 on as a research associate at the Alfried Krupp von Bohlen und Halbach Stiftungslehrstuhl für Provenienzforschung und die Geschichte des Sammelns at the Kunsthistorisches Institut of the Universität Bonn. From 2020 to 2024 she was director of the Liebermann Villa in Wannsee. Her recent publications include *Sites of Interchange: Modernism, Politics and Culture between Britain and Germany 1919–1955* (2021).

Ortrud Westheider, director of the Museum Barberini in Potsdam since 2016, completed her doctorate with a dissertation on Max Beckmann and worked at the Hamburger Kunsthalle, the Kunsthalle Bremen, and the Westfälisches Landesmuseum in Münster from 1994 to 2001. From 2002 on she was curator and from 2006 to 2016 director of the Bucerius Kunst Forum in Hamburg, where she conceived numerous exhibitions including *Max Beckmann: Menschen am Meer* (2003), *Frida Kahlo* (2006), the trilogy *150 Jahre amerikanische Kunst, 1800–1950* (2007–09), *Matisse: Menschen, Masken, Modelle* (2009), *Marc Chagall: Lebenslinien* (2010), *New York Photography, 1890–1950: Von Stieglitz bis Man Ray* (2012), *Rodtschenko: Eine neue Zeit* (2013), *Mondrian: Farbe* (2014), and *Picasso: Fenster zur Welt* (2016). At the Museum Barberini, she curated the exhibitions *Impressionism: The Art of Landscape* (2017), *Max Beckmann: The World as a Stage* (2018), *Gerhard Richter: Abstraction* (2018), *Baroque Pathways: The National Galleries Barberini Corsini in Rome* (2019), *Monet: Places* (2020), *Impressionism in Russia: Dawn of the Avant-Garde* (2020), and *Modigliani: Modern Gazes* (2024). In 2020 she curated the presentation of the permanent collection and published the book *Impressionism: The Hasso Plattner Collection.*

Daniel Zamani, artistic director of the Museum Frieder Burda in Baden-Baden since July 2024, completed his doctorate at the University of Cambridge with a dissertation on occult and medieval themes in the work of André Breton (2017). From 2015 to 2017 he was curatorial assistant and then assistant curator at the Städel Museum in Frankfurt am Main, and from 2018 to 2024 curator and head of the Impressionism collection at the Museum Barberini in Potsdam. He is coeditor of the books *Surrealism, Occultism, and Politics: In Search of the Marvellous* (2018) and *Visions of Enchantment: Occultism, Magic and Visual Culture* (2019). Zamani curated or cocurated the exhibitions *Matisse—Bonnard: "Long Live Painting!"* (2017), *Color and Light: The Neo-Impressionist Henri-Edmond Cross* (2018), *Monet: Places* (2020), *The Shape of Freedom: International Abstraction after 1945* (2022), *Surrealism and Magic: Enchanted Modernity* (2022), *Maurice de Vlaminck: Modern Art Rebel* (2024), *Yoshitomo Nara* (2024), and *Poetry of Light: Richard Pousette-Dart* (2025).

Colophon

This catalog is published on the occasion of the exhibition

Impressionism in Germany:
Max Liebermann and His Times
Museum Frieder Burda, Baden-Baden
October 3, 2025, to February 8, 2026

Avant-Garde:
Max Liebermann and Impressionism in Germany
Museum Barberini, Potsdam
February 28 to June 7, 2026

Curator in Baden-Baden:
Daniel Zamani

Curator in Potsdam:
Ortrud Westheider

Assistant Curator in Baden-Baden:
Christiane Righetti

Assistant Curator in Potsdam:
Valentina Plotnikova

Museum Frieder Burda, Baden-Baden

Managing Director: Florian Trott
Artistic Director: Daniel Zamani
Assistant to the Directors and Administration: Saskia Kohler
Head of the Frieder Burda Collection: Judith Irrgang
Research Associate for Exhibitions: Christiane Righetti
Head of Press and Public Relations/Communications: Daniela Sistermanns
Head of Digital Communications: Sophie Mattheus
Head of Finance and Accounting: Jürgen Aßmus
Events: Judith Kirschner-Forcher
Visitor Services/Administrative Assistant: Iris Haedecke
Facility Management and Exhibition Installation: Arnd Merkle, Benedikt Doll, Josef Merkel, and Ralph Vollmer
Art Workshop: Kathrin Dorfner
Concept Store: Jens Hofmann, Gertrud Geibel, and Anette Zenner
Ticket Desk: Reiner Schwarz, Susanne Dinse, and Barbara Wierzbicki
Cleaning Services: Sabine Huck

Catalog

Edited by Michael Philipp, Nerina Santorius, Ortrud Westheider, and Daniel Zamani

1st edition 2025

produktsicherheit@penguinrandomhouse.de
(The above information is mandatory information according to GPSR and should be used for all queries relating to the safety of our books)

Catalog Editing: Valentina Plotnikova and Daniel Zamani
Editorial Direction, Prestel: Markus Eisen
Graphic Design and Typesetting: BrücknerAping, Büro für Gestaltung, Bremen
Copyediting: Tas Skorupa, New York
Translations from German: Steven Lindberg, Melissa M. Thorson
Image Editing: Céline Véronique Marten, Valentina Plotnikova, and Christiane Righetti
Production Management: Cilly Klotz
Color Separations: Reproline Genceller, Germering
Printing and Binding: Printer Trento, Trento
Typeface: Neue Haas Grotesk, Lexicon No2A
Paper: 150 g/m² Garda Matt Ultra

Penguin Random House Verlagsgruppe
FSC® N001967

Printed in Italy

A CIP catalog record for this book is available from the British Library.
Library of Congress Control Number: 2025944731

ISBN 978-3-7913-7624-0
(German trade edition)
ISBN 978-3-7913-7625-7
(English trade edition)
ISBN 978-3-7913-9436-7
(German museum edition, Museum Frieder Burda, Baden-Baden)
ISBN 978-3-7913-9437-4
(English museum edition, Museum Frieder Burda, Baden-Baden)
ISBN 978-3-7913-9159-5
(German museum edition, Museum Barberini, Potsdam)
ISBN 978-3-7913-9160-1
(English museum edition, Museum Barberini, Potsdam)

www.prestel.de
www.prestel.com

Image Credits

Catalog

Museum Kunst der Westküste, Alkersum/Föhr: cats. 3, 34
Hans-Joachim Bartsch, Berlin: cats. 22, 69
Fotostudio Karen Bartsch, Berlin: cats. 53, 57
Galerie Bastian, Berlin: cats. 32, 105, 121
bpk, Berlin:
Nationalgalerie, SMB: cat. 89 • Nationalgalerie, SMB/Klaus Göken: cat. 102 • Nationalgalerie, SMB/Andres Kilger: cats. 27, 85, 86, 103 • Nationalgalerie, SMB/Jürgen Liepe: cat. 116 • Albertinum/GNM, Staatliche Kunstsammlungen Dresden/Jürgen Karpinski: cat. 9 • Hamburger Kunsthalle/Elke Walford: cats. 5, 87, 114 • Museum der bildenden Künste, Leipzig/Michael Ehritt: cat. 108 • GrandPalais Rmn/Hervé Lewandowski: cats. 28, 106 • Staatsgalerie Stuttgart: cat. 115
Kunsthalle Bremen/Lars Lohrisch/ARTOTHEK: cat. 83
Kunstsammlungen Chemnitz: cat. 128
Historisches Archiv der Stadt Köln mit Rheinischem Bildarchiv, Cologne, rba_c000964: cat. 33
Lempertz, Cologne: cats. 12, 79, 97, 123, 129
Wolfgang Fuhrmannek, Hessisches Landesmuseum Darmstadt, CC BY-SA 4.0: cats. 11, 47, 65
Galerie Ludorff, Düsseldorf: cats. 55, 63 • Achim Kukulies: cat. 56
Galerie Paffrath, Düsseldorf: cats. 100, 120
Museum Folkwang Essen/Jens Nober/ARTOTHEK: cat. 84
Städel Museum, Frankfurt am Main: cats. 7, 111
Kunstmuseum Gelsenkirchen/Martin Schmüdderich: cat. 125
Landesmuseum Hannover/ARTOTHEK: cat. 113
Staatliche Kunsthalle Karlsruhe: cats. 18, 40, 98
Galerie von Negelein, Kiel: cats. 2, 96
Tate, London: cats. 41, 104
Lübecker Museen, Museum Behnhaus Drägerhaus: cats. 8, 19, 82
Kunsthalle Mannheim/Cem Yücetas: cats. 10, 14, 44, 75
Daxer & Marschall, Munich: cat. 93
Städtische Galerie im Lenbachhaus und Kunstbau, Munich: cats. 67, 88
Kunstforum Ostdeutsche Galerie, Regensburg/Uwe Moosburger: cat. 52
Arp Museum Bahnhof Rolandseck, Remagen, courtesy private collection, Cologne: cat. 62
Stiftung Schleswig-Holsteinische Landesmuseen Schloss Gottorf, Schleswig: cat. 20
Kunstmuseum Solothurn: cat. 124
Musée d'Art moderne et contemporain de Strasbourg, M. Bertola: cat. 6
Belvedere, Vienna: cats. 17, 78 • Johannes Stoll: cat. 66
Klassik Stiftung Weimar: cat. 112
Stiftung Schlösschen im Hofgarten, Wertheim am Main/H. Hünnerkopf: cat. 95
Museum Wiesbaden/Bernd Fickert: cat. 21
Medienzentrum Wuppertal: cats. 51, 101, 107
Von der Heydt-Museum Wuppertal: cats. 39, 50
Museum im Kulturspeicher, Würzburg: cat. 71
Koller Auktionen, Zurich: cat. 45
Kunsthaus Zürich: cat. 26

Blauel Gnamm/ARTOTHEK: cat. 36
Colección Carmen Thyssen-Bornemisza: cat. 117
Grisebach GmbH: cats. 13, 59, 99
Ketterer Kunst GmbH & Co. KG: cats. 25, 38, 46, 64, 74, 76, 77
Kunsthaus Lempertz/Saša Fuis Photographie, Cologne: cat. 42
Private collection: cats. 1, 4, 16, 23, 24, 30, 31, 37, 48, 94, 118, 119, 122, 126, 127, 130, 131
Sotheby's: cat. 132
Sotheby's/Saša Fuis Photographie, Cologne: cat. 61
VAN HAM Kunstauktionen/Saša Fuis Photographie: cats. 15, 29

Axel Brachat: cats. 81, 92, 109, 110
K. Gattner: cat. 70
Lea Gryze: cat. 43
Reinhard Haider: cat. 68
Peter Hinschläger: cat. 35
Barbara Schnabel: cat. 72
Mathias Schormann: cats. 54, 60
Oliver Ziebe: cat. 80
Horst Ziegenfusz: cats. 58, 73
Jens Ziehe: cat. 91

Comparative Images

akg-images, Berlin: p. 22, fig. 1; p. 23, fig. 2; p. 28, fig. 8; p. 29, fig. 9; p. 33, fig. 3; p. 35, fig. 5; p. 38, fig. 6; p. 39, fig. 7; p. 42, fig. 1; p. 43, fig. 3; p. 44, fig. 4; p. 45, fig. 5; p. 47, fig. 6; p. 48, fig. 8; p. 48, fig. 9; p. 49, fig. 10; p. 52, fig. 1; p. 53, fig. 4; p. 54, fig. 5; p. 55, fig. 6; p. 56, fig. 7; p. 61, fig. 2; p. 96, fig. 1; p. 172, fig. 2; p. 208, fig. 1; p. 209, fig. 3 • IAM/World History Archive: p. 47, fig. 7 • National Gallery Global Limited: p. 124, fig. 2 • André Held: p. 124, fig. 1 • Erich Lessing: p. 208, fig. 2 • Laurent Lecat: p. 23, fig. 3
bpk, Berlin: Kunstbibliothek, SMB/Dietmar Katz: p. 271, fig. 6 • Nationalgalerie, SMB/Jörg P. Anders: p. 57, fig. 10; p. 172, fig. 1; p. 226, fig. 2 • Nationalgalerie, SMB/Jürgen Liepe: p. 268, fig. 4 • Staatliche Kunstsammlungen Dresden/Jürgen Karpinski: p. 43, fig. 2 • Hamburger Kunsthalle: p. 61, fig. 3 • Hamburger Kunsthalle/Elke Walford: p. 24, fig. 4 • Grand Palais Rmn/Patrice Schmidt: p. 70, fig. 1 • Museum Georg Schäfer, Schweinfurt: p. 266, fig. 2 • Lutz Braun: p. 70, fig. 2
Bridgeman Images, Berlin: p. 34, fig. 4 • Cincinnati Art Museum/Fanny Bryce Lehmer Endowment: p. 62, fig. 4 • Worcester Art Museum/Stoddard Acquisition Fund: p. 53, fig. 3 • Photo Josse: p. 97, fig. 3
Max-Liebermann-Gesellschaft Berlin: p. 267, fig. 3; p. 274, fig. 7, fig. 8; p. 275, fig. 9; p. 276, fig. 10
Ullstein Bild, Berlin: p. 277, fig. 12
Art Institute of Chicago, Public Domain: p. 152, fig. 1
Kunstpalast Düsseldorf/Horst Kolberg/ARTOTHEK: p. 266, fig. 1
CSG CIC Glasgow Museums and Libraries Collections: p. 27, fig. 6
Walter Bayer/NEUMEISTER Münchner Kunstauktionshaus GmbH & Co. KG, Munich: p. 57, fig. 9
Metropolitan Museum of Art, New York, Public Domain: p. 25, fig. 5; p. 27, fig. 7; p. 60, fig. 1; p. 66, fig. 6
Philadelphia Museum of Art, Public Domain: p. 32, fig. 2
Portland Art Museum, Public Domain: p. 97, fig. 2
Hasso Plattner Collection, Museum Barberini, Potsdam: p. 32, fig. 1; p. 52, fig. 2; p. 190, fig. 1; p. 191, fig. 2
National Gallery of Art, Washington, Public Domain: p. 56, fig. 8; p. 63, fig. 5; p. 125, fig. 3; p. 153, fig. 2; p. 173, fig. 3; p. 226, fig. 1
Kunsthaus Zürich: p. 227, fig. 3

Grisebach GmbH: p. 276, fig. 11
Simonis & Buunk Fine Paintings, Ede, the Netherlands: p. 71, fig. 3
Wikipedia Commons, Public Domain: p. 270, fig. 5
Wildenstein Plattner Institute, Inc.: p. 67, fig. 8

Image has been reproduced from the following publication: Philippe Cézanne, *Paul Cézanne dépeint par ses contemporains,* Lyon 2021, p. 215: p. 66, fig. 7.

Image details have been used on the following pages: pp. 2–3 (cat. 120), pp. 4–5 (cat. 47), pp. 6–7 (cat. 126), pp. 8–9 (cat. 44), p. 12 (cat. 86), p. 14 (cat. 79), p. 20 (cat. 115), p. 25 (cat. 7), p. 30 (cat. 102), p. 36 (cat. 12), p. 40 (cat. 82), p. 46 (cat. 8), p. 50 (cat. 77), p. 58 (cat. 132), p. 64 (cat. 131), p. 68 (cat. 7), p. 94 (cat. 43), p. 122 (cat. 63), p. 150 (cat. 66), p. 170 (cat. 87), p. 188 (cat. 100), p. 206 (cat. 114), p. 224 (cat. 130), p. 256 (cat. 93), p. 264 (cat. 104), p. 269 (cat. 117), and p. 272 (cat. 132).